Jean Baudrillard and Radical Education Theory

Brill Guides to Scholarship in Education

The titles published in this series are listed at *brill.com/bgse*

Jean Baudrillard and Radical Education Theory

Turning Right to Go Left

By

Kip Kline and Kristopher Holland

BRILL

SENSE

LEIDEN | BOSTON

Cover illustration: Image by Kristopher Holland

All chapters in this book have undergone peer review.

The Library of Congress Cataloging-in-Publication Data is available online at http://catalog.loc.gov

Typeface for the Latin, Greek, and Cyrillic scripts: "Brill". See and download: brill.com/brill-typeface.

ISSN 2590-1958
ISBN 978-90-04-44535-2 (paperback)
ISBN 978-90-04-44536-9 (hardback)
ISBN 978-90-04-44537-6 (e-book)

Contents

Foreword

Jean Baudrillard (1929–2007) was a French philosopher whose work has found a new relevance today. He died before the financial crash of 2008 and before the COVID-19 pandemic, yet his particular vision of a world punctuated by these kinds of crisis continues to be illuminating. In this new book by Kline and Holland it is this particular reading of the crisis of culture in the Western world as it concerns education which is in focus. There are thus two elements here, first Baudrillard's own general theory of this crisis, and secondly Baudrillard's relevance to method and practice. In both of these aspects of his writings and activities Baudrillard radically reverses many deeply and closely held basic assumptions of educationalists.

The first reversal concerns the crisis itself: for example the world seems no longer to be one that is under human control (if it ever was), but a world that is de-regulated in all major aspects. Baudrillard explores this de-regulation in surprising analyses of post-modern forms of virtuality from Disneyfication to computer generated imagery as a basic problem of how to think the very basic term: reality as it too becomes de-regulated. His analyses of hyperreality, virtual reality, and absolute reality have been widely influential. The first reversal is to think through the proposition that the dialectical world of counter-balances has been superseded by one that had gone to extreme logics in every domain as an effect of the sovereignty of the object. And these logics now have to be considered as challenges threatening the very existence of humanity itself.

A second reversal concerns modern technology, particularly communication and media technology. Very simply it can be asked whether this is an extension of the human organism, a system of tools employed to carry out tasks defined by the human subject, or whether these technologies hijack these projects and hold them hostage. Baudrillard's approach here is to suggest that the logic of these technologies is one that goes towards an extreme, the complex process of exclusion of the human. The question thus reposed is: what is the new relation between the human and the inhuman in a modern world dominated by sophisticated communication technologies? It could certainly be argued that modern educational systems have been revolutionised by these technologies over the last fifty years and that these now hold the practices of education in hostage. The traditional practices of human contact and oral transmission of cultures have been replaced gradually by a pervasive virtualisation through television, computer, smartphone. What has happened is a unification of media: phone, radio, television, typewriter, and camera. And the consequence is the world is now instantaneously both more real and more virtual. Instead of an alienation effect here, Baudrillard argues, the new problem is absorption and immersion, and the loss of critical distance.

As the authors of this new book argue Baudrillard does not suggest the solution to these problems lies in a return to a promethean vision, to the sovereignty of the subject, to a new mode of production. His writings call for a re-evaluation of issues around symbolic cultural forms and a new relation to the object for those able to place themselves in symbolic exile from the new machine, call taken up by Kline and Holland in a fine lucid exploration and discussion.

Mike Gane
Emeritus Professor of Sociology
Loughborough University
August 22, 2020

Make Friends with Chaos in Chaotic Times

> But no vision of America makes sense without this reversal of our values: it is Disneyland that is authentic here! The cinema and TV are America's reality! The freeways, the Safeways, the skylines, speed and deserts – these are America, not galleries, churches, and culture.
>
> BAUDRILLARD, (1989, p. 104)

∴

Kip Kline and Kristopher Holland's Guide, *Jean Baudrillard and Radical Education Theory: Turning Right to Go Left* arrives at a dangerous and chaotic point in history and we are thrilled to have it in the series because in numerous ways it becomes imperative to understand our current reality and whether it is reality. This is the fourth addition to the Guides already in the series. It focuses on an individual's work and the impacts that work has on education. Other Guides include David Backer's volume entitled, *The Gold and the Dross: Althusser for Educators* (2019), *Key Scholarship in Media Literacy: David Buckingham* by Allison T. Butler (forthcoming) and Derek Ford's *Inhuman Educations: Jean-François Lyotard, Pedagogy, and Thought* (forthcoming). The series, Brill Guides to Scholarship in Education are short introductions to various fields and scholars in education and fields related to education written for experts and novices. Though sophisticated in content, the style of these books is less structured or restricted than existing guides taking a novel approach, they can be used as an educational tool in undergraduate and graduate courses as introductory texts. This is particularly true for the Kline and Holland Guide.

We are facing a global pandemic with COVID-19 and nothing seems stable or certain anymore. It could be described as a chaotic nightmare. In America we can't even shop for groceries at Safeway or Wal-Mart any longer without face masks. It often is reminiscent of many post-apocalyptic movies. We can also decide to have those items delivered to our homes or our cars in the store's parking lots. In public schools and universities the entire "normal" has been disrupted. In some states in schools and universities students are experiencing modified face to face classes or classes on Zoom or some hybrid version of both. Perhaps, Zoom needs to be added somewhere in Baudrillard's reality/

simulacra analysis. It is a time of nightmarish chaos. Reality seems to be ever-changing or even unreal. The authors address this chaos in this text.

> Instead truth circulates, it is never tethered to anything – like conspiracy theories and pyramid schemes which have become 'reality' in our context. This results is a certain kind of chaos. And Berardi (2019) says, "Those who wage war on chaos will be defeated because chaos feeds upon war … chaos is stronger than order. So the best thing to do is to make friends with chaos" (pp. 1–3). This is the task of the philosopher of education as fatal theorist and fatal strategist. (p. 69)

The discussion of reality and chaos are certainly relevant to the current historical moment and we welcome the author's work on these topics. *Jean Baudrillard and Radical Education Theory: Turning Right to Go Left* is an outstanding addition to the series. We are sure you will find the Guide informative and enlightening.

Reference

Baudrillard, J. (1989). *America*. Verso Books.

William M. Reynolds and Brad Porfilio

Figures

About the Authors

Kip Kline

(1971) is a philosopher of education and lives in Forest Park, Illinois. He is currently Interim Dean of the College of Education and Social Sciences at Lewis University in Romeoville, Illinois where he oversees the departments of education, justice, law, and public safety studies, political science, psychology, social work, and sociology. He has been a professor at Lewis since 2007. Dr. Kline holds a Ph.D. in philosophy of education from Indiana University.

The focus of his work is philosophy of childhood and adolescence with an emphasis on film, media and technology, postmodernism, and futurism. He has written two monographs, one edited volume, several refereed journal articles and book chapters, and given dozens of papers at peer-reviewed research conferences. He serves on the editorial board of *Educational Theory*.

Dr. Kline delivered an invited talk at the University of Sheffield in 2018 at the Philosophy and Education Symposium, Humanities Research Institute. In 2017, he was the invited speaker at the Philosophy and Education Colloquium, Teachers College, Columbia University, New York where he delivered an address on his first book on Jean Baudrillard. In 2010, he gave an invited lecture at the Department for Aesthetics, Aarhus University, in Aarhus, Denmark.

Before attending graduate school, Kip Kline spent five years teaching high school English in Ohio and Indiana.

Kristopher Holland

(1977) is an artist and philosopher living in Cincinnati, Ohio. He is a Professor of Art and Design Education in the College of Design, Architecture, Art, and Planning (DAAP) at the University of Cincinnati. He received his M.A. from

New York University, and his Ph.D. in Philosophy and Art Education from Indiana University.

He is the Director of the Strange Tools Research Lab at the Digital Futures research collaborative and the Director of Visual Arts & Design Education State Licensure for the University of Cincinnati. He is also the director of Art and Publications for the Žižekian Institute for Research, Inquiry, and Pedagogy. As a visiting professor at the Karl Franzens University's Institut für Kunstgeschichte in Graz, Austria he teaches courses on a range of subjects including: Joseph Beuys, The Vienna (& Berlin) Secession, Baroque Art and Theories of Knowledge, Philosophy of Technology, The Black Radical Tradition, Conceptual Art, Object Orientated Ontology, and Political Theory as Art Production.

Dr. Holland current research interests are: philosophical inquiry methodologies, arts-based research, art & design teacher education, deconstruction, contemporary art and critical theory. He has recently given guest lectures at the New York University Steinhardt School of Culture, Education, and Human Development on the topic of Jean Baudrillard and 'Post-Art' and at the Ringvorlesung with the KUWI Graz consortium in Austria on the topics: "The Ignorant Artist: Post-Politics and Aesthetic Education" and "Introducing Strange Tools." He is presently researching the role inquiry plays in educational curriculum within PK-12 Schooling with projects connected to Hughes STEM High School and the Nelson Mandela International School in Berlin, Germany. He collaboratively ran an afterschool arts-based inquiry program and participated in the Hughes STEM HS Summer Scholars Program as a curriculum advisor and educator from 2012-2018. He also co-directs the biannual Berlin Summer Studio Arts Inquiry program in collaboration with the Weißensee Kunsthochschule Berlin.

His conceptual work of art, *The Habermas Machine*, was cited in James Rolling Jr.'s Arts-Based Research: A Primer, published in 2013 and was exhibited in 2015. In addition to the co-authored book *Jean Baudrillard and Radical Education Theory: Turning Right to Go Left* for Brill, his work appears in publications such as: *The Journal of French and Francophone Philosophy* [*Revue de la philosophie française et de langue française*], *Visual Arts Research Journal, The Journal of Social Theory in Art Education, Studies in Art Education*, and the *International Journal of Žižek Studies*. By combining the fields of philosophy, art, and education, his work seeks to spark agency for students in the creative fields for social change and educative innovation.

The Seduction of Baudrillard

Jean Baudrillard's ideas are conspicuously absent from most educational literature. Often when they are obliquely referenced, they are misrepresented and sometimes even sabotaged. For example, Douglas Kellner and Jeff Share engaged with Baudrillard's ideas in the context of media literacy and education, but this work is incongruent with Baudrillard's context of third and fourth orders of simulacrum (Kline, 2016a). As is the case in other treatments of Baudrillard, Kellner and Share's incomplete reading of Baudrillard leads to mischaracterization at best and caricaturization at worst. Although he is included in some handbooks of educational theory, particularly those with discussions of postmodernism and poststructuralism, Baudrillard usually serves as a straw man to either illustrate or articulate a displeasure with the postmodern condition (which, ironically, Baudrillard shared) (van Kessel & Kline, 2019). Some educational theorists have earnestly engaged Baudrillard's ideas, such as his critiques of contemporary capitalism. One prominent example is Trevor Norris (2011).

One of the aims of this guidebook is for it to serve as part of a corrective effort to push back on the under- and misuse of Baudrillard in educational theory in general and in philosophy of education specifically. Because we are convinced that his virtual omission from the literature in philosophy of education is a mistake worth correcting, we introduce him here as an important figure in radical thought who has something to add to our theoretical lines of inquiry in education. Since we have both been drawn to Baudrillard in the context of philosophy of education, we are committed to an effort of providing a more prominent place for Baudrillard's ideas in radical theoretical conversations in education.

We start by briefly tracing our individual histories with Baudrillard's ideas and provide general, introductory arguments about his usefulness to philosophy of education. Baudrillard's writing has elicited strong reactions (and we include the reaction of dismissal here) for decades. The content of his arguments, his style, the trajectory of his *oeuvre*, all stand out as distinct, even in the bounded range of late 20th and early 21st century critics of modernity. The nearest to a home discipline we can assign to Baudrillard is sociology, given his formal academic training and experience, but it is hardly debatable that Baudrillard practiced philosophy. In particular, his was an applied philosophy, drawing on not just sociology but media theory, gender studies, cultural theory,

© KONINKLIJKE BRILL NV, LEIDEN, 2021 | DOI: 10.1163/9789004445376_001

economics, art, and other disciplines in order to mete out his descriptive arguments and critiques of the state of human beings, objects, capital, media, film,
television in late modernity. His work traversed a prodigious amount of literature in all of these disciplines and was expressed using language from all of
them (even sometimes borrowing specialized terms from the natural sciences,
particularly biology). Not unlike philosophy of education itself (as a field),
Baudrillard's writing was multi-disciplinary and therefore was both widely
appealing and widely disturbing. As scholars in a field of interdisciplinarity,
we now discuss our own paths to becoming scholars of Baudrillard.

1   Baudrillard's Teaching: How I Learned to Avoid the Trap of the
         Dialectic
         (Kip Kline)

A Ph.D. in philosophy of education is necessarily an interdisciplinary degree.
My course of study in graduate school included not only philosophy but sociology as applied to educational thought, critical methodology, religious studies,
and so on. The range of ideas and thinkers I was exposed to was wide and
somewhat unconventional. But my philosophical focus in grad school was
American pragmatism – specifically the neopragmatists (e.g., Rorty, Bernstein,
West). I was attracted for two primary reasons. The first is found in Richard
Bernstein's (1989) address to the American Philosophical Association in 1988 in
which he described 'the pragmatic ethos.' Of the five themes he offered as con-
stituting this ethos, I was particularly drawn to 'anti-foundationalism' and 'rad-
ical contingency.' Bernstein traced these themes back to Peirce and Dewey but
I eventually understood them as a bridge to postmodernism/post-structuralism
and to a certain iteration of what is now called anti-philosophy, particularly as
it has been located in Nietzsche and Wittgenstein by Badiou (2011).[1] To be clear,
Bernstein, clearly understood there to be a through-line between the original
American pragmatists to postmodernism. Bernstein begins by using a term the
American pragmatists didn't – 'anti-foundationalism.' He argues that a series of
Peirce's papers in 1868 "presents a battery of arguments directed against the idea
that knowledge rests on fixed foundations, and that we possess a special faculty of
insight or intuition by which we can know these foundations" (Bernstein, 2013).
Bernstein recognizes this as an adumbration of a critique that later become
known as 'the metaphysics of presence.' This critique had a number of itera-
tions in the 20th Century, not the least of which was Derrida's critique of Husserl in *Speech and Phenomena* in 1967 (Derrida & Allison, 1984).

I was also attracted to Cornel West's use of pragmatism as social and cultural critique, particularly in *The American Evasion of Philosophy* (1989). Taken together, these neopragmatist ideas gave me a taste for a kind of *radical critique* and that eventually led me straight to Jean Baudrillard, who, redefined the concept of radical thought and critique for me. Although he was a trained sociologist, from my first reading I found his ideas to be decidedly philosophical and, contrary to a number of what I now consider misreadings, I have found a clear, systematic philosophy in his works (and certainly plenty of others consider his writings as works of philosophy).[2]

Originally, I was interested in (as most readers of Baudrillard are, at least, initially) the ideas of hyperreality, the loss of the real, and simulation theory. My initial understandings of these ideas are as follows. Disneyland, mega shopping malls, television sports spectacles are all examples of the better, the more intense than 'everyday life' that constitute the domain of the hyperreal. Hyperreality is complicit in the disappearance of reality or, put another way, reality is displaced by the hyperreal. Unfortunately, the popular notion that the film *The Matrix* is illustrative of Baudrillard's simulation theory is wrong. At least it's wrong according to Baudrillard. He said, *The Matrix* is the sort of film the Matrix would have made about the Matrix(!). He later claimed, "The most embarrassing part of the film is that the new problem posed by simulation is confused with its classical, Platonic treatment. This is a serious flaw" (Genosko & Bryx, 2004, n.p.). That is, the world of 'the perfect crime' that leaves no trace is decidedly *not* the world of Plato's Cave. In that world, it is still possible to locate the distinction between the illusory world of the images on the wall and the real world outside of the cave. Baudrillard's provocative claims are not meant to describe a complete fall into illusion, on the contrary. In the simulated world, there is no more illusion. Everything is transparent. Everything is actualized.

As my study of Baudrillard progressed, I gravitated toward his commentary on the end of dialectical critique and his concept of radical thought and critique. In what he calls the fourth order of simulacra, the era of complete virtuality, as well as simulated, 'cool' forms of communication, the capitalist code and the ubiquity of the screen (image) conspire together to swallow up dialectical forms of critique. In fact, critique (traditional/dialectical) is encouraged in the late capitalist code but it is quickly subsumed into another set of signs for consumption (see, for example, Kline, 2016b, p. 33).

Of course, this is but a gloss of my encounter with Baudrillard's writing. The point is that I became entirely convinced that Jean Baudrillard is a useful figure to introduce (in a systematic way) to the field of philosophy of education and in particular to what could be referred to as the critical strand of philosophy of education. That is, those who find contemporary conditions of schooling or discourses about youth lamentable, those who critique *prima facie* aims of education, the corporatization of schools and universities, etc. often seem to be employing the kind of critique that Baudrillard claims has become impotent in the late 20th century and beyond.

In making use of Baudrillard's radical critique in philosophy of education, I found it necessary to explain to colleagues my motivation for doing so. I was aligning myself with those who think it is possible that the clock on modernity's central projects has run out. And by extension, I think it may be fair to wonder if, for those of us concerned about the plight of youth and education broadly speaking, it is time to look elsewhere than critical theory or John Dewey's democratic education or dialectical critique in general for both our philosophical descriptions of and responses to the more lamentable conditions of our contemporary moment and their relationship with education.

It is for these reasons that I turned to Baudrillard, who claimed that dialectical critique is inefficacious in contemporary times in which the semiotic has fully displaced the symbolic [by symbolic he means that which is outside of the capitalist code and outside of representation – the "privileging of an immediately actualized, collective mode of relations and its transformative experience and communication" (Merrin, 2006, p. 12)]. "All forms that tend to project a dazzling and miraculous liberty are only revolutionary homilies," he said (Baudrillard, 2008, p. 184). Traditional forms of resistance, based in critical or emancipatory theories are only capable of producing *signs* of resistance. This is the problem posed by late capitalism. The late capitalist code is adept at subsuming critique and offering it back as a set of signs to be consumed. As mentioned above, the code actually encourages a certain level of critique. The perennial example here (and perhaps too well-worn) is the Che Guevara t-shirt but in the social media/internet age we can think of a litany of new ways in which capitalism encourages a certain level of critique that it then recuperates, in the sociological sense, and it often does so in multiple layers. The last scene of the popular period (1960s) television show on the U.S.'s AMC channel, *Mad Men*, comes to mind here as well. After a long series of both professional and existential battles, the show's protagonist and anti-hero, Don Draper, advertising's creative genius *par excellence*, finally seems to begin to find some kind of inner peace at a hippie commune in 1970. Then, as he's seated in a group of people doing yoga exercises somewhere on the California coast, he gets the inspiration for the iconic 1971 Coca-Cola 'Hilltop' advertisement – "I'd like to buy the world a Coke." There are many layers of recuperation and simulation happening here. There is the 'real' 1971 Coca-Cola advertisement that recuperated the peace movement as a means of selling soda. Then we have the final

scene of a television show that *simulates* that recuperation. Beyond those simulations and recuperations, the entire show itself is a series of simulations that
recuperates certain resistance movements in the 1960s and turns them into a
consumer resurgence of mid-century modern styles in furniture and fashion
on the strength of the popularity of the show. Baudrillard saw this kind of thing
coming – a screenified world in which layers of simulation and recuperation
would fold onto each other *ad infinitum.*

The examples above also suggest that effective resistance cannot be dialectical because synthesis or resolution is the very dynamic of the capitalist
system as it constantly reinvents itself through the sign code. Another way of
putting this is that critique is rapidly absorbed by simulation. So, again, I am a
Baudrillardian scholar in large part because I have lost faith in the efficacy of
modern forms of critique in late capitalism. This loss of faith in what I will call
traditional critique is a primary motivation for promoting the study of Baudrillardian ideas in educational theory. If we are concerned with critiquing the
status quo of educational institutions, their relationship to late capitalism, critiquing contemporary discourse about youth, etc., we must also be concerned
with the efficacy of our critique vis-à-vis the late capitalist code.

Both my journey to Baudrillard scholarship and my view of his importance
to philosophy of education are informed by his facility for near-future anticipa-
tion (and much of that which he anticipated has demonstrably been realized),
his response to that which he was anticipating, and the way it might be useful
for theorists of education. In short, Baudrillard offers critical philosophers of
education a new way of responding to lamentable conditions – with enigma
and counter-intuition, that is, turning right to go left.

> The world was given to us as something enigmatic and unintelligible, and
> the task of thought is to make it, if possible, even more enigmatic and
> unintelligible. (Baudrillard, 2012, p. 199)

This kind of radical thought may be a way out of the trap set for critical theory and other forms of dialectical critique by the late capitalist code and the
ubiquity of the image. At least, this is in part what this book will argue in the
context of educational theory.

I owe this understanding of Baudrillard to a host of remarkable scholars
who have come before me and who have produced indispensable secondary
literature on Baudrillard's work. I cannot mention them all here but, William
Pawlett's (2007) book has seminally influenced my overall reading of Baudrillard. Gary Genosko's (1999) work on Baudrillard and McLuhan and William
Merrin's (2006) more recent text on Baudrillard and the media have been
highly influential in my own Baudrillard scholarship. My book on Baudrillard

and the depiction of youth in American film would not have happened without the work of the late Gerry Coulter, founding editor of the *International Journal of Baudrillard Studies*.[3] Finally, Mike Gane's entire corpus on Baudrillard is and continues to be both a key underpinning of and inspiration for my own work. These fine Baudrillard scholars have been personally gracious to me and incredibly supportive of my efforts to carve out a space for Baudrillard in philosophy of education.

2   9/11 Did Not Take Place: Or How I *Learned* to Love Baudrillard
         (Kristopher Holland)

It seems that this obsession with the passage to action today governs all our behavior: obsession with every real, with every real event, with every real violence, with every pleasure which is too real. Against this obsession with the real we have created a gigantic apparatus of simulation which allows us to pass to the act "in vitro" (this is true even of procreation). We

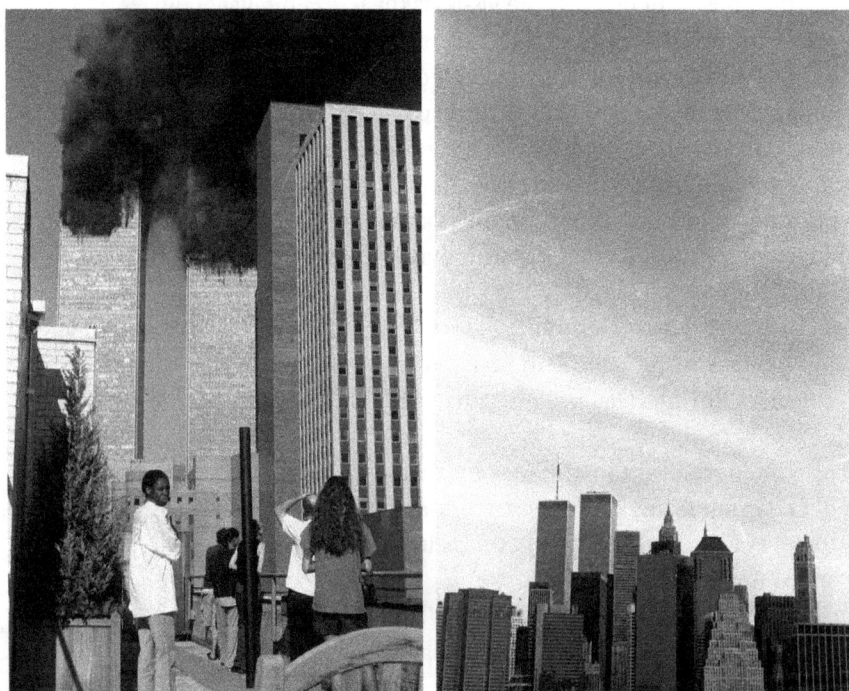

FIGURE 1   Two photos of Twin Towers. Left: From roof deck of 99 John Street, September 11, 2001. Right: From Brooklyn Heights, September 9, 2001
PHOTOGRAPHS: © KRISTOPHER HOLLAND

prefer the exile of the virtual, of which television is the universal mirror, to the catastrophe of the real. (Baudrillard, 1995, p. 28)

By the grace of terrorism, the World Trade Center has become the world's most beautiful building .... (Baudrillard, 2002, p. 37)

I have a roll of black and white film, which I loaded into my camera September 9, 2001 that contains an interesting string of images – two of which are pictured in Figure 1. I had just moved into my student housing which was located at 99 John Street to begin my graduate school program. That weekend, I began to take photographs of my new surroundings and fall into the city. On a vacant Sunday afternoon, September 9th, I walked from my apartment across the Brooklyn Bridge and took a few pictures of the lower Manhattan Skyline. On Tuesday, September 11 that roll of film was completed.

Looking back on the events of 9/11, I can see my interest in Jean Baudrillard's ideas were ignited. But this spark was not instant. In fact, it took a few years for me to first discover Baudrillard as a thinker, and then many years to develop an understanding of his complex notions. But once I did grasp his radical flavor for philosophical style (admittedly in English translations) I was enamored with the style *and* substance of his work. This was appealing to me as an artist who constantly struggles with connecting style and substance of complex ideas. Baudrillard would be important for that reason, but also because in his work I found a kindred spirit for the reflections on the events of 9/11.

What I remember from 9/11 is from direct experience, or what I think most would call 'reality.' I saw with my own eyes the second plane hit the building, the fireball, and the eventual collapse of both towers. Interestingly, one of my first childhood memories is ash or the gray 'snow' falling from the Mt. St. Helens eruption in 1980. That was an equally aesthetic and profound sight one never forgets. 9/11 would also create gray ash which snowed down that evening along with paper ephemera and poisons galore from the destruction. The physical proximity of my apartment was so close to the maelstrom that I was not allowed to return to my home that night. As a walked across the Brooklyn bridge on my way an acquaintance's house, I kept staring at the smoldering lights and hearing the incessant noises at what would eventually be called ground zero. The sky was a smoldering color as the night arrived. Papers were still floating around in the air and the smell or burnt plastics, soot, and what I would call general New York dust overcame my senses. As I arrived as my friend's house, the T.V. light was visible through the window, and I encountered 9/11 for the first time.

The next day, I slipped the exclusion zone at Houston Street with the help of a cop who only asked my zip code (10003). I then walked through the inches of ash, trudged up to the 19th floor of my building to my apartment and gathered a few things. I had yet to absorb the previous day's events. But what I immediately recognized was the media version I had encountered at my friend's house was not connecting with my experience. I felt uneasy as everywhere I went the event was playing non-stop on every screen. I would come to understand in hindsight that I was experiencing deterrence. In fact, 9/11 made me *feel* the concept of deterrence. Having experienced this event, I felt powerless, unsure, 'deterred' from processing and understanding it. Importantly here is when Baudrillard's thought became an experience for me. If simulation deters reality, then this for me was a realization that the modeling or coding of 9/11 had begun. This simulation was what greeted me everywhere I went for the next few years as people found out I 'was there.' But where was I on 9/11?

I want to evoke 9/11 in this introduction because one of the points I wish to make about Baudrillard's thought is that it is applicable to everyday life. This is the potential power of his thought and especially his style of presenting it. But we must tread carefully as Kline notes above. The misreadings of Baudrillard's ideas (possibly stemming from his style) have resulted in his work being written off as 'not philosophy' – whatever that means forty years after Richard Rorty exposed this pseudo-problem which seems to infect philosophy of education as a field.[4] Our argument in this book is that to properly encounter Baudrillard is useful to philosophy of education, and this text aims to demonstrate his anti-philosophy for our field through an introduction of his thought and how it can be applied.

Returning to my experience of the World Trade Center event, I began to realize in the weeks and months that followed that my experience entered the realm of mediation and memory. As I absorbed the media narrative or code '9/11,' my memory and experience began to be re-written, recoded, and assaulted by a displaced reality. What I would later come to verbalize using Baudrillard's ideas, and to paraphrase Kline above, is that my 'reality was displaced by the hyperreal' – the 'real' version of 9/11 which did not match my lived one. The World Trade Center event was already, even as it was happening, being transformed, mutated into something for those in the world outside of the direct experience of it into '9/11.' In a sense 9/11 was constantly being 'actualized' to me, as feedbacks of mediated footage slowly began replacing all of our memories in repetition. Everything was now revealed in the footage of reality, my reality became infected, polluted forever by the 'actual' footage of the 9/11 – henceforth there was no illusion, I could simply pull up the news archives and relive the events at any time.

As the weeks flew by, my milieu in New York was conditioned by 9/11 in most of my interactions with people. I eventually returned to live at my student housing at 99 John Street in lower Manhattan. Every day I left for class I would pass by the rubble, smell the burnt plastic, and be blinded by the star bright wielding of metal. This became an important daily ritual in forming my thoughts on 9/11. What I continued to experience was a gap between what I was experiencing as someone in the lower Manhattan neighborhood, and how people told me what I experienced based on their mediated version. I would go to class with people who lived elsewhere and they would speak in knowing ways about how the ground zero site was going, and how the city had forever changed – all from their mediated perches. Again the 'deterrence affect' was beginning to have the effect of me questioning my own experiences. Each day I was struck by the multiple takes on the event I began to get from the media and others in my program, including my family who all watched it on TV. 9/11 began to fractal out into interrelated realities. Instead of the telephone game, we now had the 'internet game.' The internet version of the telephone game is faster and allows global mangling of information. I began to feel more and more uneasy about the whole event, as the way I witnessed it with my own eyes and continued to experience the aftermath living near ground zero without a screen was different from most people (which is still a phenomenon I experience twenty years later).

At the risk of being insensitive, I must admit that, for me, the World Trade Center event was one of the most beautiful things I have ever seen. The crisp sky, the nervous energy, the sense of dread, the huge plane flying into the building, the fireball and sound concussion delay – all things I will never experience again. The burning buildings, the rumble of the collapses, the 'snow' of gray ash, and walking around with random paper pieces falling around, have all become memories seared into my neurological history. But given the general mood regarding these things and 9/11, I kept these aesthetic impulses to myself.

Given these candid memories, I became annoyed with representations of the event as '9/11' from the start. From the crass T-shirts and sweatshop merchandise, to the Bush administration's use of the event to plug us into the war code, the machine of history began writing in a certain style, a branding operation of sorts, only 'respect' for the event was permissible – the code was forming. It seemed to me that watching the event from multiple footage angles like American football game replay leitmotif became a snuff film. Not only for conspiracy theorists, but the general public. The media constantly showed the destruction of the twin towers and Pentagon. Either in real time, or for the dissection of documentary connoisseurs in order to order truth.

Make no mistake, it was a tragic day, it was terrorism, etc. But to me – seeing it in real life – it had a sort of beauty – and when I read the essay by Jean Baudrillard of which I quoted from at the beginning of this section, I began my encounter another person who in my mind spoke to my troubles for 9/11.

We must never forget the power of singular events, especially if there is an aesthetic quality to them. Singular aesthetic events like the World Trade Center collapse change lives. That another person admitted there was beauty in this event gave me an intellectual rush. Baudrillard's essay *The Spirit of Terrorism* first appeared in *Le Monde* November 3, 2001. When I finally encountered this essay, it really connected a lot of thoughts I had about the attack, the coding of the event as 9/11, and much more. During the months after the event I had become interested in reflecting and seeing 9/11 in the context of American Empire. On my first pass of the essay I agreed with much of the points Baudrillard was making. To me, when my friends began to ask 'why do they hate us,' I was always trying to explain our faults in the international world order and critique American empire. This connected to Baudrillard's essay when he says: "This is what particularly frightens us: the fact that they have become rich (they have all the necessary resources) without ceasing to wish to destroy us" (Baudrillard, 2002, p. 18). We had seemingly exported globalization and 'prosperity' all over the world – the new world order of Bush (both Bush's – more on the Gulf War soon) was supposed to make everyone happy according to the logic of neoliberal capitalism. No matter, certain people still wished to destroy us because all that prosperity was a ruse. The truth of American empire, and neoliberal reorganization was proven hollow as Baudrillard (2002) continues: "Admittedly, their deaths prove nothing, but in a system where truth itself is elusive (or do we claim to possess it?), there is nothing to prove" (p. 18). Here Baudrillard began to speak at a deeper level to me, and I was interested in following his ideas further.

As I re-read the essay, I began to get more out of it. Baudrillard's discussion of the radicalization of the image to reality helped me get beyond the simplistic critique of American Empire and begin to connect to how I was experiencing my reality with the construction of the event 9/11. This event, which in a sense *became* 9/11 to people, was following a certain logic of image. As Baudrillard writes:

> The role of images is highly ambiguous. For, at the same time as they exalt the event, they also take it hostage. They serve to multiply it to infinity and, at the same time, they are a diversion and a neutralization. The image consumes the event, in the sense that it absorbs it and offers it for

consumption. Admittedly, it gives it unprecedented impact, but impact as image-event. (Baudrillard, 2002, p. 21)

To me this captures my experience of the World Trade Center event with the emergent '9/11 image-event' into a philosophical description.

Furthermore, Baudrillard (2002) writes:

> In this case, then, the real is superadded to the image like a bonus of terror, like an additional frisson: not only is it terrifying, but, what is more, it is real. Rather than the violence of the real being there first, and the frisson of the image being added to it, the image is there first, and the frisson of the real is added. Something like an additional fiction, a fiction surpassing fiction. (p. 22)

Here we have for me the real connection of Baudrillard to my everyday life, as a function and logic of the image – which in our screen mediated (learning) culture must be theorized. This is how I learned to live with '9/11.' This is why his work is important to consider for education and experience – a focus of the field of philosophy of education.

Given this positive reading of Baudrillard's work, my interest in his other writings continued to grow as I became a high school art teacher in East New York Brooklyn. Teaching art and design to high school students post-9/11 was when I began to consider that the ways in which we represent reality, the ways in which signs and ideologies of the day mediate events and produce a certain 'code' of memory. As Baudrillard (2002) states:

> We try retrospectively to impose some kind of meaning to it, to find some kind of interpretation. But there is none. And it is the radicality of the spectacle, the brutality of the spectacle, which alone is original and irreducible. (p. 23)

My students also lived through the World Trade Center event, but it was hard for us all to resist the code of 9/11. This 9/11 code seemed to be more important than the reality of the event. For most of us, the 9/11 code was, indeed, swapped out for the event. I began to study Baudrillard's other works in more detail and started to make connections that for me pointed to a radical rupture with how we critique reality.

As we entered another war in the Middle East, I re-read Baudrillard's essay on the first Gulf war – where he famously claims it 'did not take place.' "The real victory of the simulators of war is to have drawn everyone into this rotten simulation" (Baudrillard, 1995, p. 59). It seems as though we were repeating history, but this time with 9/11 laying the groundwork for the new code of reality from which society and culture would be created. I kept coming back to Baudrillard's notions of symbolic, simulation, and reality. I remember sitting in my room, during the breaks in teaching and looking out the window towards the Manhattan skyline and thinking how quickly the event of The World Trade Center was now impossibly erased and replaced by another version (9/11) that justified what would become the war on terror.

To get out of the trap reality has set for us, we need radical theory – and Baudrillard has addressed this in multiple ways. In simulation all signs, images etc., are without origin – 9/11 – doesn't need an origin – as it was not real – the World Trade Center event happened, but 9/11 was a 'map that proceeded the territory,' it was an event created after the event, which is not the real event. We can no longer find the real 9/11! In the same sense of the Gulf War, *9/11 n'a pas en lieu* .... As Kline alludes to in the first section, dialectical forms of critique are not going to give us back reality – the real 9/11 is a simulation – the World Trade Center event I saw is now polluted memories, mixed into the endless re-conditioning by the code '9/11' – instead the sign of critique will always replace critique itself. Baudrillard saw this in the first Gulf War, and now again with '9/11.'

The War on Terrorism seems to be a deeper and radically more flagrant version of The Gulf War, or the model of the gulf war being the war on terror. The outcome is pre-determined – the war cannot be lost since it has no origin and is not 'real.' "Since this war was won in advance, we will never know what it would have been like had it existed" (Baudrillard, 1995, p. 61). If the Gulf war was simulated by computers and outcomes known in advance through algorithms, the War of Terror seems to be an even more powerful simulation (we will examine in Chapter 3 how Disneyworld is a 'deeper simulation' of Disneyland). Our drone bombings, technological capture of entire cultures, the entrapment of domestic terrorists, etc., actually creates more future terrorists – it is *the map of the war on terror creating the (territory of the) war on terror.* We have created a descent into the simulation, the war of terror moves us even further from the catastrophe of the real, we have already forgotten the origin because there is none. The 'code' of the war on Terror is found everywhere, and it has become an all-consuming part of the self and political-economic engine or model for our age. To paraphrase Kline from earlier in this text – resistance to this age cannot be dialectical.

After encountering Baudrillard's work in the way I sketched above, I realized that there is a contemporary moment that is different than before. We need a different set of theoretical tools to address our age. The Gulf War, 9/11, the War of Terror did not take place, what we have instead are advertising campaigns.

What happened for me that day September 11, 2001 was seen with my eyes, and taken in a few photographs has now forever been short-circuited, mediated by the constant re-remembering and images of the event (including my own and this introduction). Thus, the branding of 9/11 was an operation that was in full swing even as the moment unfolded. The nature of news, T.V., the internet, representation itself was turned over to simulation some time ago. As Baudrillard (2002) writes: "It is not 'real.' In a sense, it is worse: it is symbolic" (pp. 22–23). He goes on the say "... the media are part of the event, they are part of the terror, and they work in both directions" (p. 24). We need to come to grips with the notion that we prefer illusions to reality. This has been true in the West since (if not before) the ancient Greeks stopped making realistic statues and began to idealize the human form.[5] So what type of world is it when everything is actualized, when there is no more illusion?

I began to think about fatal strategy in dealing with my deterrence. I had the alibi of being there. I had the alibi of Baudrillard's thought. But what to do? What can be done? Baudrillard (1995) gave me a clue from his text on the Gulf War when he states:

> Resist the probability of any image or information whatever. Be more virtual than events themselves, do not seek to re-establish the truth, we do not have the means, but do not be duped, and to that end re-immerse the war and all information in the virtuality from whence they come. Turn deterrence back against itself. Be meteorologically sensitive to stupidity. (pp. 66–67)

Here we have Baudrillard's fatal strategy – turn deterrence back on itself (which will be addressed in Chapter 4). Through Baudrillard I had to come to grips with learning 9/11 did not take place, and in doing so realized the value his radical thought can have for our times.

This text will investigate Baudrillard's work for a radical educational theory, one that exposes counter-paths, disappearance, and fatal strategies for educational theory. It is in no way a comprehensive introduction to Baudrillard's ideas. That has been done very well by Mike Gane (1995), William Pawlett (2007), and others. Instead we introduce and analyze Baudrillard for the specific purpose of establishing his use, relevance, challenge, and promise to educational theory. In so doing, we necessarily omit important sections of his *oeuvre* and we proceed in a nonlinear fashion. This guidebook ultimately asks the following question: In a realm of simulated education, what is to be done? Chapter 1 will examine Baudrillard's relevance for educational theory. Chapter 2 presents the failure of critical forms of educational theory and practice to address the urgent concerns linked to the unfolding catastrophes of our age. Chapter 3 gives a post-mortem on representation and describes the age of simulation, and Chapter 4 announces fatal strategies and theory for education.

Notes

1   There are, no doubt, some pragmatists who would argue that American pragmatism does not necessarily provide a philosophical bridge to postmodernism in general or to antiphilosophy in particular. I have no real interest in engaging that argument here since the primary point is that my *interest* in Baudrillard is connected to my study of neopragmatism.
2   In particular, Mike Gane has located a system in Baudrillard's writing (see Gane, 1995).
3   https://baudrillardstudies.ubishops.ca/
4   See Richard Rorty's (1979) book *Philosophy and the Mirror of Nature* for his brilliant counter to analytic philosophy's claim to 'proper' philosophical discourse.
5   See Nigel Spivey's documentary, *How Art Made the World*.

References

Badiou, A. (2011). *Wittgenstein's antiphilosophy*. Verso.

Baudrillard, J. (1995). *The Gulf War did not take place*. Power Publications.

Baudrillard, J. (2002). *The spirit of terrorism*. Verso Books.

Baudrillard, J. (2008). *Fatal strategies*. Semiotext(e).

Baudrillard, J. (2012). *Impossible exchange*. Verso.

Bernstein, R. J. (1989). Pragmatism, pluralism and the healing of wounds. *Proceedings and Addresses of the American Philosophical Association, 63*(3), 5–18. doi:10.2307/3130079

Bernstein, R. J. (2013). Pragmatism, pluralism, and the healing of wounds. *American Philosophical Association Centennial Series, 2013,* 601–615. https://doi.org/10.5840/apapa2013182

Derrida, J., & Allison, D. B. (1984). *Speech and phenomena: And other essays on Husserl's theory of signs*. Northwestern University Press.

Gane, M. (1995). *Baudrillard: Critical and fatal theory*. Routledge.

Genosko, G. (1999). *McLuhan and Baudrillard: Masters of implosion*. Routledge.

Genosko, G., & Bryx, A. (2004). The matrix decoded: Le Nouvel Observateur interview with Jean Baudrillard. *International Journal of Baudrillard Studies, 1*(2). http://www.ubishops.ca/baudrillardstudies/vol1_2/genosko.htm

Kline, K. (2016a). Jean Baudrillard and the limits of critical media literacy. *Educational Theory, 66*(5), 641–656. doi:10.1111/edth.12203

Kline, K. (2016b). *Baudrillard, youth, and American film: Fatal theory and education*. Lexington Books.

Merrin, W. (2006). *Baudrillard and the media: A critical introduction*. Polity Press.

Norris, T. (2011). *Consuming schools: Commercialism and the end of politics*. University of Toronto Press.

Pawlett, W. (2007). *Jean Baudrillard: Against banality*. Routledge.

Rorty, R. (1979). *Philosophy and the mirror of nature*. Princeton University Press.

van Kessel, C., & Kline, K. (2019). "If you can't tell, does it matter?" Westworld, the murder of the real, and 21st century schooling. *Journal of Curriculum and Pedagogy*. doi:10.1080/15505170.2018.1542358

West, C. (1989). *The American evasion of philosophy: A genealogy of pragmatism (The Wisconsin project on American writers)*. University of Wisconsin Press.

CHAPTER 1

Relevance for Educational Thinking

When announcing Baudrillard's relevance for educational thinking, it is useful to address how his style of writing, how he wants us to experience his philosophy, wades into the *possibility of thinking*, or the radical potential for thinking itself. In this chapter we will describe how Baudrillard's work functions as a counter to the code of education, rational thought, critical reason, etc. In effect, we will establish that which Badurillard advocates for a counter-path to thinking that can shake us out of our ready-made thoughts and realize the radical potential for change.

1   **What Does Baudrillard Say about Thinking? Paradox in Baudrillard as Productive Spaces for Learning**

Let us take a moment to analyze this work of art by Allan D'Arcangelo in Figure 2 known by some as the modern artist of highways and signs. As one encounters this 'sign' (as reproduced on this paper – reducing the size, altering the scale and context, etc.) there is a descriptive and metaphorical trajectory we will connect to what we refer to as 'Baudrillardian space.' We will use 'Baudrillardian space' to refer to moments, signs, events, etc. that can help us discover the productive potential in his thought – or put it to work – here found in 'the Trip.'

In a descriptive sense, *The Trip* (1963) is a screen-print of an arrow symbol (pink) pointing left, and a symbol for a right hand (in yellow) pointing right. The colors are bold and bright on white background framed as a square – connecting to what the artist sees as the significance of road signs in American culture. In an empirical sense, the sign would be a curious and perhaps confusing road sign if actually placed on a road or actually used to help navigate a city scape.

Moving beyond this descriptive code, we can imagine a few questions that move us into a speculative narrative. Is this a 'real' road sign? Where would one encounter it? How should it be read? In the text, *Learning from Las Vegas* (1977), which is an analysis of the 'symbolic' in architecture, signs, landscapes, *the reality of Vegas of late 1960's*, we find this work of art placed by the authors in the book to describe the current state of Las Vegas. The authors of the book see Vegas as a metaphor for time and place in the West in general, where origins, previous 'encoding' of what is and is 'not' a cityscape – the roads, advertising,

© KONINKLIJKE BRILL NV, LEIDEN, 2021 | DOI: 10.1163/9789004445376_002

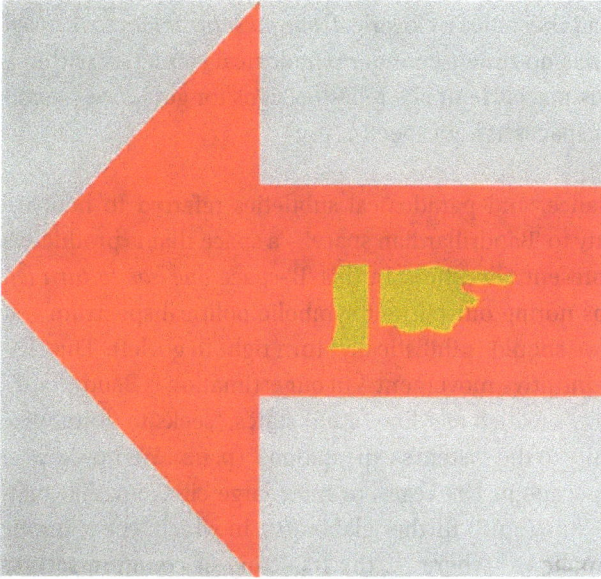

FIGURE 2   *The Trip* by Allan D'Arcangelo (1963, as cited in Venturi et al., 1977)

store fronts, etc. – has been eroded, the previous boundary markers that signify 'city' have 'disappeared.'

Thus the city itself is now overcome in the spectacular fight for the human perceptive apparatus by the plethora of signs and new information cluttering the space and time of anyone trying to navigate it. In the (future) city, of which Las Vegas is a case study, the symbolic in space and time has replaced the other modes of reality construction. We now must navigate through the signs of city in order to try and make sense of a 'real' Las Vegas. The signs as types of maps proceed the empirical territory of cities.

Perhaps deeper still, Venturi et al. (1977) find in encountering the sign city of Vegas a cancellation of previously learned codes for how to consume signs themselves. *In Vegas one is inundated by signs relaying not information on how to navigate the landscape, but as interruptions in one's ability to navigate.* This is a key shift in interpretation of the reality of signs and codes in life. In Vegas the idea of sign itself was transformed, or better yet, transferred into a new code – one that sees signs as a continuous assault on the senses in order to reorientation the system, to make you leave previous 'realities' – in order to bring you to the reality of Las Vegas. In navigating this new landscape of hyper-signage and confusion a new 'logic' is created – *one must turn left in order to go right*, rightly captured by the artist.

In the *Learning from Las Vegas* text, Venturi et al. (1977) comment on D'Arcangelo's 'road sign' as follows:

> When the crossroads becomes a cloverleaf, *one must turn right to turn left*
> ... But the driver has no time to ponder paradoxical subtleties within a
> dangerous, sinuous maze. He or she relies on signs for guidance – enor-
> mous signs in vast spaces at high speeds. (p. 9)

The high speeds, guidance, and paradoxical subtleties referred to here we
would argue link directly to 'Baudrillardian space' – a space that is productive
for encountering our present condition. In this 'B'-space *one has to turn left
to go right* – or perhaps noting our current symbolic political spectrum – it
might be better to say we should (nihilistically) turn right to go 'left.' This diz-
zying concept, counter-intuitive movement – in our estimation is Baudrillard's
search for a fatal strategy – which as Kline (2016) states, "seeks to destabilize
through hyper conformity to the system's expectations" (p. 112). We now *expect*
a confusing urban sign-scape in Las Vegas, or most large cities for that matter. This is a world, as Kline (2016) further elaborates, in which "the semiotic
has colonized the symbolic ...," where "... the trajectory of communications
technology has substituted virtual non-communication for proximal human
interaction ..." and "... the deluge of signs without referents – a word of simulations [has] supplanted the dialectical relationship between illusion and the
real" (p. 114). The dialectic, or claims to a dialectical shifting of reality in order
to understand it, has disappeared. Reality shifting, in Baudrillardian space,
instead of being a linear dialectic, is now a counter-spiral – turning right/left
to 'go' left/right. This is indeed a process, like a dialctic, but as we will see later
in this text in detail, describes a different operation altogether. While this way
of encountering reality was not birthed in Vegas alone, it is indeed upon us in
late modernity.

    The assertion that Vegas represents a Baudrillardian space is important as
it connects his thought to lived reality. Or perhaps better put a 'tactical awareness' of how reality now functions. The Baudrillardian 'tactical awareness' sets
up benchmarks and/or strategic objectives in order to combat our current situation. We must always understand that this Baudrillardian call is not about
more 'rational resistance' practices, or Marxist liberation theologies. Instead
of the classic liberation strategies, when confronted with the new function of
reality we must seek radical thought and fatal theories in order to unravel – or
perhaps –re-ravel the order of experience (reality). In Kline's words: "In the
place of a Marxist theory of resistance, Baudrillard offers fatal theory and radical thought" (2016, p. 118). Thus, the new order of reality alluded to in 'the Trip'
(as cited in Venturi, Scott Brown, & Izenour, 1977) and the 'Las Vegas reality' –
needs new forms of resistance.

If Baudrillardian radical thought is opposed to critical thought (and it fol-lows that this applies to thought in the field of education and, indeed, in the very idea of education) then this assertion leaves us with questions and work to do. What is a radical thought? How do we wield it? What are the repercus-sions in abandoning critical thought in education? Without the space and time to address each one of these questions we would like to simply ask at this point, what can we learn from 'stranger' places (see Noë, 2015, for more on use of strange tools in this area) – where reality is going right to turn left – what aspirations can we hope for in fatal strategies?

Perhaps the biggest shortcoming in Baudrillard's work is that it does not fit into rationalist or critical discourse so frequently evoked in philosophy of edu-cation (and other fields). Simply put, this Baudrillardian space makes it hard to present his work in a format, code, or system – such as an argument, pub-lished paper, dialectic, or even dialogical (e.g., in education, Paulo Freire) dis-course. For Baudrillard the space of critical thought itself has disappeared. And although some critics fully missed this point, this disappearance was not a pos-tivie development for Baudrillard. As Kline (2016) puts it, Baudrillard thought of late modernity as: "… a world of too much reality and objectivity, not a lack of it, a world of full actualization. Hyperreality constitutes this world in which reality lacks nothing and all negation has been subsumed. And here is no lon-ger any critical thought" (p. 120). Perhaps it's like trying to write about art – we can with words evoke trajectories of thought – but art works such as *The Trip* need a certain 'sighting' or a way to experience them outside of 'critical thinking' – which will always come up short in capturing artistic experience. Perhaps one should always respond to art with art – evoking the infamous phrase: 'writing about music [art] is like *dancing about architecture ...*'

This is also the strength of the Baudrillard's work and necessitates a certain tolerance for novelty, nonlinearity, counter-intuition (a la quantum physics), and paradox frequently found in artistic, poetic, and even theoretical physics outlets. The question is: is our society, culture, and education discourse even capable of reading this type discourse outside its 'own terms' (writing about architecture)? Can 'fatal theories' be read without the codes of rationality sub-suming them? (and) Once we can read these 'fatal strategies' can we stay away from containment and reasoning – can we avoid 'dancing about architecture'? In other words, can philosophy (as a rational critical discourse) read Baudril-lard? Can one even 'do' Baudrillardian theory within the constriants of linear, critical discourse styles?

These are important questions we must countenance here. In our interpre-tation of Baudrillard it is a blessing and a curse found in his work and requires a delicate 'dance' when writing about his ideas. When reading his books, the careful treading is noticed and appreciated – we get the 'feeling' he was dancing about architecture – but fully aware this dance was trying to lead us to discover radical writings as a productive force (Baudrillard's way of naming this process was 'theory-fiction'). We would like to speculate what learning might be in the context described – what can we both learn *from* and *with* Baudrillard? And how can we learn from and with Baudrillard in philosophy of education?

2   Imagining 'Learning' from Baudrillard

> Roadside copies of Ed Stone are more interesting than the real Ed Stone. (Venturi et al., 1977, p. 8)[1]

This, we think, is the best quote from *Learning From Las Vegas* and connects wonderfully to Baudrillard's call for new strategies of resistance. Admittedly this quote outside of the world of architecture might mean nothing – who is Ed Stone? Why do architects laugh at this dig from the text and the rest of us stare into the abyss or run to Google to find out who he is? That is precisely why it is effective here. Does one even need to know Ed Stone? Does one need to know who he is in this context to get 'it'? The structure of the argument – the structure of the sentence is more important – Roadside copies of 'x' are more interesting than the real 'x.' Roadside copies of McDonald's are more interesting than the real McDonald's. We can already believe the copy (copies) are more interesting than 'the real' – we already believe in the reality of the copy as 'more interesting' – we have already been implicated in the code Baudrillard is so worried about.

Baudrillard's work has a certain 'counter-spiral,' much like turning left to go right in *The Trip* sign presented in Figure 2. Kline (2016) writes: "Baudrillard's theory of resistance aims to avoid the inscription of the rationality of the system and to circumvent neutralization in the code" (p. 119). Here we have the last and perhaps most important point in exploring Baudrillard in the sphere of a strategy of resistance, or anti-philosophy; namely Baudrillard doesn't celebrate this code of simulation, but instead critiques it – albeit with a new strategy of critique. We must 'undergo' the hyperreality in order to 'overcome' it.

This logic evokes others who practice a philosophy of counter spirls. One example is the philosophy of Dominique Janicaud. Much of Janicaud's (2002/ 2005) work focuses on the technological question, over use of rationality, and human nature. He puts forth the notion that in order to change the conditions of humanity we should not double down on rationality and technology, which is what 'overcoming' reality means, but instead celebrate the irrational and 'human' aspects of living (undergoing). But the key movement here is that in order to get back to an authentic undergoing of life, we need to undergo the ultra-rationalization of lifeworlds. In Janicaud we have a quasi-Baudrillardian strategy here of 'undergoing' the rational changes in society until they implode and we realize that we need to 'overcome the drive to overcome.' This is a logic that tries to teach us *undergoing* is a way to 'move right to go left.'

In connecting Baudrillard to the *Learning from Las Vegas* text in terms of it educative function we would also like to harp on the use of the word 'learning.' As the featured section quotation by Venturi et al. alluded to – the copy of Ed Stone is more interesting that 'real' Ed Stone buildings. The code of Ed Stone's architecture is recognized all around the country – we learn it without schooling. This learned code, this 'code' is the type of reality (its the one we have – which is theoretically one of many possibilities) that Baudrillard sees all around us – even in the 'architecture of education.' At the end of his text on Baudrillard, Kline (2016) leaves us with a call to imagine the accompanying education required to counter-act our code of neoliberalism, testing, 'homo-economicus' drivers (human nature as purely 'rational self-interested individual) that underwrites the educational complex today. We need to combat that code, combat 'Ed Stone's architecture in education' and re-write – or 'dance' the educational theories that can point out $\Rightarrow^2$ the obscenity of 'truths' in an objective, over rationalized society, a society lost to signs without origin, where each McDonald's on the side of the road are all more interesting that any 'original' (indeed there is a trend to make some McDonald's restaurants look like the 'original hamburger stand' – evoking/simulating nostalgia). We need to imagine an education that points out that 'order' that addresses the educational code without allowing the previous 'Marxist critical frameworks' to overwrite our resistance. We need an education theory *that moves right to go left.*

Baudrillard's work has a bearing on education in general and media and art education specifically. We would be remiss to not consider the points expressed in his work and should immediately embark on a project of fatal theory – radical thought – (which will be addressed in Chapter 4). But before we arrive there, we have a few loose ends that need to be explored in terms of education.

3   The Ecstasy of Education

In addition to finding Baudrillard's relevance to philosophy of education in his radical ideas about thinking in general, we also find Baudrillard's concept of ecstasy particularly relevant to educational thinking. To set the context, we begin with a lengthy quote from the 20th century Romanian philosopher, Emil Cioran (1949/2012):

> No wavering mind, infected with Hamletism, was ever pernicious: the principle of evil lies in the will's tension, in the incapacity for quietism, in the Promethean megalomania of a race that bursts with ideals, that explodes with its convictions, and that in return for having forsaken doubt and sloth – vices nobler than all its virtues – has taken the path to perdition, into history, that indecent alloy of banality and apocalypse ... Here certitudes abound: suppress them, best of all suppress their consequences, and you will recover paradise. (p. 4)

Our view in this guidebook is that Baudrillard's work defends the value of enigma, illusion, indeterminacy, myth, and the secret. We then take the further step of claiming that it, indeed, defends their *educational* value. Terms such as 'the secret' and its concomitant ideas are mostly out of vogue in contemporary society and even, perhaps, particularly in educational discourse and practice. Some scholars have gone so far as to say that whispering, the great engine of the secret, is becoming (has become?) obsolete in the stage of surveillance the world has reached something beyond panopticism and synopticism to something like a 'superopticon' in which we are all surveilling each other and ourselves constantly and we have come to expect that we are probably being recorded (read: watched) in some form or another at all times. A reversal of this situation requires the valuing of enigma, illusion, indeterminacy, etc. To say that these things have value is, we think, counterintuitive to most and this captures one of the primary reasons why we suggest there is great value in using Baudrillardian ideas to promote counter-intuitive thinking in education.

A brief sketch of a recent political exchange in the U.S. is instructive with regard to the need to infuse education with counter-intuition. Not long ago on one of the Sunday political television shows in the U.S., Rudy Giuliani, in his role as the head of Donald Trump's legal team, said in the midst of an exchange with *Meet the Press*'s Chuck Todd, "... truth isn't truth ..." (NBC News, 2018). Democrats and other Trump critics seized on the sound bite without providing context (the television exchange, of course, does not lend itself to exploring context anyway) to mock another in a series of speech acts in which Trump associates are ostensibly out of touch with 'reality.' The phenomenon began early in the Trump administration when Kellyanne Conway, Counselor to the President, infamously used the phrase "alternative facts" in a television interview to argue in favor of Trump's clearly inaccurate claim about the size of the crowd at his inauguration (NBC News, 2017). To be clear, this is not in any

way an attempt to defend anyone in or anything about the Trump administration. It seems perfectly obvious to us and presumably most readers of this
book that Trump and several of his associates trade in outrageous lies (and this
is, of course, just the beginning of the epistemological problems with Trump).
But we are much more interested for the purposes of the context for the arguments here in the response to these claims of Trump associates by the American Left (which, we argue, has dissolved into what we would traditionally refer
to as liberals). In the case of Kellyanne Conway's locution, "alternative facts,"
a prodigious amount of voices on the Left responded in both traditional and
social media outlets. Most of the pushback did not explicitly accuse Conway
or Trump of lying *per se* but rather mocked Conway's particular articulation
as an affront to the definition of the term 'fact' as though the primary offense
here was the violation of a fidelity to objectivity. The Left had mostly a similar response to Giuliani's "truth isn't truth" sound bite. How appalling that
he question the absolute nature of truth?! The Left seems to think this kind
of statement is worthy of unrelenting derision. To be clear again, we are not
claiming that Conway and Giuliani are not deserving of derision. On the contrary. And yet these responses to them by the Left are, in our view, a problem.
Is the Left now committed to the notion of immutable fact? Is it committed
to a positivist, objective notion of truth? Never mind that Giuliani probably
meant (if taken in full context) something that might have been defended by
the American pragmatists in the early to mid-20th century. Another way of
understanding this might be that the Left's response reveals its commitment
to the late-Enlightenment version of pursuit of certainty and a belief in and
attachment to determinacy. It might be that the Left has simply gone in with
the rest of the world for excessive information, excessive visibility, excessive
certainty.

   In his later work, Baudrillard (see Gane, 2000, for an overview) made
descriptive arguments about the world in which he highlighted its radical
uncertainty. The sheer volume of information available in the late (post)mod-
ern world turns out, perhaps counterintuitively, to negatively affect what we
know. For example, in pharmacology, despite the technology development
since the mid-20th century that has allowed for the collection and testing of
massive amounts of data, the production of new drugs has steadily declined
throughout the same time period. Eroom's law is what this phenomenon is
called in pharmacological research but the idea has a wider range of applica-
bility when taken together with Baudrillard's arguments about the loss of the
comforting world of determinacy and certainty. Specifically, Baudrillard was
concerned with the diminishing returns of a world in which everything is visible, everything is transparent. He also consistently said that accepting radical

uncertainty and, indeed, responding to the enigmatic world with *more* enigma, was preferable to a relentless (and doomed) pursuit of empirical certainty. In educational discourse and policy, almost without exception, the usefulness of the pursuit of empirical certainty, of new pedagogical technology, of big data, is presumed (see Boyles & Kline, 2018; Muller, 2018). Specific parts of Baudrillard's corpus can help to expose the problems of such pursuit in education and also provide ideas regarding the amelioration of those problems. In short, Baudrillard's concept of ecstatic forms are useful in forwarding the need for a robust concept of counter-intuition in educational discourse and theory.

In the 1980s Baudrillard began to write of the end of the dialectic of meaning. Things no longer derive meaning from their opposites but rather elude the dialectic and potentialize themselves into extremes and into obscenity. The result is that we now are left with ecstatic forms. These ecstatic forms are the result of things no longer being relative their opposites and they are thus "caught in an intensifying spiral – more true than true, more beautiful than beautiful, more real than the real – [and are] assured a vertiginous effect that is independent of all content or specific quality ..." (Baudrillard, 1990, p. 27). Things then become superlative, Baudrillard claims, as if they have consumed all the energy of their opposite. When truth has absorbed all of the energy of the false, the result is simulation; when beauty has absorbed all the energy of ugliness, the result is fashion, he says by way of examples. And this is precisely what he means by ecstatic forms, "that quality specific to each body that spirals in on itself until it has lost all meaning, and thus radiates a pure and empty form" (Baudrillard, 1990, p. 28).

The most familiar of the examples above is the phenomenon of truth absorbing all the energy of the false that results in simulation. Baudrillard discusses this in the context of film. With film and/or cinema, he laments the loss of illusion. He claims that illusion was a central feature in the cinema of his youth. But far from simply feeling nostalgic about these films, he understands the loss of illusion in films – that happens through the technical perfection of the image – to result in hyperreal films in which the real is no longer locatable. Baudrillard (1994) stated,

> The cinema and the imaginary (the novelistic, the mythical, unreality, including the delirious use of its own technique) used to have a lively, dialectical, full, dramatic relation. The relation that is now being formed today between the cinema and the real is an inverse, negative relation: it results from the loss of specificity of one and of the other. (p. 47)

We are, then, able to call it ecstatic cinema today.

Baudrillard mentions a number of examples of ecstatic forms and he includes what he calls 'anti-pedagogy' which is the pure and empty form of pedagogy. He does not say anything more about the ecstatic form of pedagogy so that is where we can begin to flesh out the ideas surrounding the need for a concept of a counter-intuition in education. What might we say about the ecstatic form of pedagogy and what arguments can be made about this idea relative to educational discourse and practice? Perhaps we can reflect on the existence today of a strict, technical-oriented concept of pedagogy having fully realized itself in fairly recent phenomena such as highly scripted lessons in which for-profit entities have essentially 'teacher-proofed' the 'learning' of students in K-12 institutions. With it, we have the concomitant notion of 'fidelity' in which classroom teachers are often pressured through both positive and negative incentives to, in effect, 'stick to the script.'

A very recent phenomenon in teacher preparation in the U.S. is instructive here. Since the COVID-19 pandemic spread across the U.S. in the spring term for colleges and universities (the term during which most teacher education students complete their student teaching practice and also complete some form of standardized teacher preparation assessment) and for K-12 schools, it became impossible for teacher education students to complete their student teaching. When K-12 schools closed and provided instead 'remote learning,' college students in their final semester of teacher preparation could not go into schools to student teach. Some state boards of education (which, in the U.S. are the licensing bodies for teachers) waived the requirement for student teaching and for the teacher preparation assessment. We are not arguing here for or against this move made by state boards of education, rather, we are recounting this phenomenon in the context of ecstatic pedagogy to suggest that the move was, in part, a tacit admission that pedagogy has been 'teacher-proofed' in the U.S. and no egregious harm will come of new teachers not having had the advantage of student teaching. We have developed a perfected (and also empty) form of pedagogy that only requires fidelity to the script.

This pursuit of the most exacting form of pedagogy, aimed at removing any shred of uncertainty is surely what Baudrillard would call ecstatic. In a society that has come to intuit and eventually presume the value of the pursuit of eradicating uncertainty, perfecting everything, multiplying and categorizing everything until all things have fully realized themselves, it is no wonder that we have developed an ecstatic form of pedagogy. It is difficult to say exactly what we would mean by the opposite of pedagogy. But if it could be something like teaching without method or education without method (or intention?) then we can safely conclude that much pedagogy today has absorbed all the energy of its opposite. It has become disassociated from its opposite. Not just in the example of scripted lessons and the concept of fidelity, but we also find this disassociation in the expectation that teachers write copious amounts of lesson plans that they are required to turn into administrators. This surely is a form of pedagogy that aims to seal any possible crack of undecidedness and eliminate anything impromptu or unexpected. Indeed, it is a form of pedagogy that renders these concepts obsolete. Ecstatic pedagogy is pedagogy that absorbs all of the energy of education without method – if that is anything like the opposite of pedagogy. And when it does so, it becomes pure and empty. Although the world of educational policy may have intuited that pursuing this kind of pedagogy is preferable to a pedagogy that maintains an association with its opposite, the incidence of what is being referred to as 'teacher burnout' is on the rise (Santoro, 2018). No doubt, some of these disillusioned teachers are affected by the ecstatic forms of pedagogy that are foisted upon them.

We can also locate ecstatic pedagogy in the presumption on the part of many educators of the inherent value of new technological gadgetry marketed to assist in the pedagogical process. The use of 'smart boards' (or other visual/ internet technology) in classrooms, electronic tablets for students, and other forms of video and computer-based 'learning tools' are not just ubiquitous in schools but their value is unequivocally presumed and almost never challenged. This is even the case for so many involved in teacher education at universities. The presumption of the value of technology to education has become so intensely assumed that, combined with the late capitalist code, it has produced a new kind of educator altogether – the tech brand teacher. *The New York Times* (Singer, 2017) recently reported on a North Dakota teacher, Kayla Delzer, who embodies Silicon Valley's penchant for all things techno-education. She is a 'teacher-influencer' who has her own so-called 'brand' and receives financial benefits by making referrals to high-tech firms and education entrepreneurs.

Education start-ups like Seesaw give her their premium classroom technology as well as swag like T-shirts or freebies for the teachers who attend her workshops. She agrees to use their products in her classroom and give the companies feedback. And she recommends their wares to thousands of teachers who follow her on social media (Singer, 2017). As she puts it, "I will embed it [new technologies] in my brand every day" (Singer, 2017, para. 4). The commercial and ethical issues this raises are only indicative of the (logical?) consequences that follow from this kind of technophilia. But more to the point of our arguments here, the very condition of the existence of this 'teacher as ed tech brand' is ecstatic forms of pedagogy and education. Both the teacher/ brand, Delzer, and the ed tech entrepreneurs with whom she works constitute a constellation in which fully realized late capital education and pedagogy exist. The same article introduces us to Nicholas Provenzano, a teacher in suburban

Detroit who, according to Singer (2017), "... consults for education technology companies, and his basement is chock-full of the electronics they send him to try" (para. 16). The article goes on to say that "... he used a $1,299 3-D printer sent to him by Dremel, a tool brand for which he is an ambassador, to turn his students' designs into three-dimensional objects. He printed one student's design, a gavel, representing the struggle for justice in the novel [*To Kill a Mockingbird*]" (Singer, 2017, para. 28). With regard to the activity of 'representing the struggle for justice' in *To Kill a Mockingbird* it seems fair to ask what educational advantages there are in making a gavel out of polycarbonate in a $1300 3-D printer over making one, say, out of papier-mâché for a few cents. But this is an impossible question to ask in the era of ecstatic pedagogy. No one will hear it.

Whether we locate them in the technical perfection of pedagogy through gadgetry or the intersection of teachers as brand and the 'ed tech' industry or through the exacting nature of fidelity to pre-scripted lessons (or elsewhere), ecstatic forms of pedagogy permeate the practice of education. But it has also become intuitive to create ecstatic forms of educational discourse. It is very difficult to gain any traction in contemporary society with educational discourse that does not derive from the notion of a perfected trajectory of school to university to high paying job. In universities, many scholars, even in the arts and humanities, have surrendered to making instrumental arguments for their importance. A humanities or an arts education is important because employers value humanities-oriented skills (or, as humanities and social science skills have become in recent parlance, 'soft skills'). We must make the argument this way. We have no choice. No one will understand or listen to a non-instrumental argument for the value of the humanities.

4   Toward an Education for Counter-Intuition

> To the more true than true we will oppose the more false than false. We will not oppose the beautiful and the ugly; we will seek what is more ugly than the ugly: the monstrous. We will not oppose the visible to the hidden; we will seek what is more hidden than hidden: the secret. (Baudrillard, 1990, p. 7)

This is one way that Baudrillard explains what he calls fatal strategies (discussed in more detail in Chapter 4). If we are going to learn to enact these counter-intuitive forms of opposition, we must have an education for counter-intuition.

Baudrillard has his own articulation of Eroom's Law. While Eroom's Law is confined to drug development slowing and becoming more expensive over the same time that technology has improved and developed, Baudrillard's (1990) is perhaps a more general epistemological statement when he discusses a U.S. report on the oil company, Exxon:

> [T]he American government requests a complete report on the multinational's activities throughout the world. The result is twelve 1,000 page volumes, whose reading alone, not to mention the analysis, would exceed a few years work. Where is the information? (p. 190)

Ecstatic forms of information/knowledge yield no information/knowledge. Baudrillard (1990) then provides a clue for the development of an education for counter-intuition when he asks, "Should we initiate an information dietetics? Should we thin out the obese, the obese systems, and create institutions to uninform?" (Poster, 1988, p. 190). Yes, we should. We should create institutions that teach counter-intuition in order to oppose the enigmatic quality of the world not with clarity but with more enigma. Such institutions would have to reverse the disarticulation of exacting pedagogy from teaching without method. They would need to teach toward the opposition of 'obese systems' and teach toward the 'thinning out' of information.

Because we have learned to intuit the value of an infinite drive toward empirical certainty and because we have learned that we must pursue a virtual liberation through technology and in this way, achieve utopian subjectivity, we have developed ecstatic forms of pedagogy and education. These ecstatic forms have reinscribed the intuition just mentioned. In order to reverse it, we must imagine an education for counter-intuition. We must begin to teach and not to oppose our uncertain and enigmatic world with an insatiable drive for empirical certainty but with more uncertainty and more enigma. And instead of pursuing a fully realized (virtual), liberated subjectivity, we must learn and teach in such a way to begin to find a path of radical strangeness. Otherwise we are doomed not just to the metastasis of identity, a self that repeats itself forever, but also to technological teachers-as-brand no doubt begetting students-as-(tech) brand. Otherwise we are doomed to ecstatic (read: meaningless) forms of education and pedagogy.

Notes

1   Ed Stone is perhaps the most hated architect of the modern era. See the following article for more background: https://lareviewofbooks.org/article/the-most-hated-of-architects-on-edward-durrell-stone/ and see also Wolfe (1981).
2   Derridian digression of the arrow in the text – the arrow is seen, not heard – toward Derrida's radical thought – fatal strategy of writing.

References

Baudrillard, J. (1990). *Fatal strategies*. Semiotext(e).

Baudrillard, J. (1994). *Simulacra and simulation*. University of Michigan Press.

Boyles, D., & Kline, K. (2018). On the technology fetish in education: Ellul, Baudrillard, and the end of humanity. *Philosophical Studies in Education, 49*, 58–66.

Cioran, E. M. (2012). *A short history of decay*. Arcade Publishing. (Original work published in 1949)

Gane, M. (2000). *Jean Baudrillard: In radical uncertainty*. Pluto Press.

Janicaud, D. (2005). *On the human condition* [*L'homme va-t-il dépasser l'humain? (Will man overcome the human?)*] (E. Brennan, Trans.). Routledge. (Original work published in 2002)

Kline, K. (2016). *Baudrillard, youth, and American film*. Lexington Books.

Muller, J. Z. (2018). *The tyranny of metrics*. Princeton University Press.

NBC News. (2017, January 22). *Kellyanne Conway: Press secretary Sean Spicer gave 'alternative facts' meet the press NBC News* [Video]. YouTube. https://www.youtube.com/watch?v=VSrEEDQgFc8

NBC News. (2018, August 19). *Rudy Guiliani: 'Truth isn't truth' meet the press NBC News* [Video]. YouTube. https://www.youtube.com/watch?v=CljsZ7lgbtw

Noë, A. (2015). *Strange tools: Art and human nature*. Hill and Wang.

Poster, M. (1988). *Jean Baudrillard, selected writings*. Stanford University Press.

Santoro, D. (2018). *Demoralized: Why teachers leave the profession they love and how they can stay*. Harvard Education Press.

Singer, N. (2017, September 2). Education disrupted: Silicon Valley courts brand-name teachers, raising ethics issues. *New York Times*. https://www.nytimes.com/2017/09/02/technology/silicon-valley-teachers-tech.html?mcubz=0&_r=0

Venturi, R., Scott Brown, D., & Izenour, S. (1977). *Learning from Las Vegas: The forgotten symbolism of architectural form*. MIT Press.

Wolfe, T. (1981). *From Bauhaus to our house*. Picador.

CHAPTER 2

The End of Traditional Critique in Education

1   The State of Critique in Education

There is currently no shortage of critique in academic scholarship in education. The 2019 annual meeting of the American Educational Research Association was organized around the following theme – "Leveraging Educational Research in a Post-Truth Era: Multimodal Narratives to Democratize Evidence." In the frontmatter of the program, this theme is explained, beginning with epigraphs from Hannah Arendt on totalitarianism and W. E. B. DuBois on slavery. AERA's opening paragraph (2019) explains the recent rise in popularity of the term 'post-truth' and then goes on to say,

> Indeed, we see daily examples of policy issues – from climate change to immigration – in which appeals by powerful leaders to personal beliefs and emotions hold more sway than objective facts and evidence. And while DuBois reminds us that 'evidence' has also served racist agendas under the guise of objectivity, in the current political context, lies and misinformation coupled with what Arendt calls 'contempt for facts' by powerful leaders regularly incite fear, hatred, and White supremacist protests, such as the one in Charlottesville, VA, in August 2017. (Wells, Jellison Holme, & Scott, 2019, para. 1)

Here, we can see that one of the most powerful organizations in academic research in education has backed itself into an aporetic situation owing to its thinly veiled connection to the modern disorders of hyper-rationality, objectivity, and arithmomania that operate explicitly and in the midst of its critique. Even more revealing is the admission of the President and Co-Chairs of the organization that the material products of such disorders, or what they call "research evidence," can just as easily be used for ill as it can for good; can be adopted, rejected, obfuscated, championed, decontextualized, and so on. This admission becomes clear as Wells, Jellison Holme, and Scott (2019) first start with the Du Bois epigraph and then call further attention to it and emphasize the existence of, "racist agendas under the guise of objectivity" (para. 1). But, they nonetheless drop this particular concern about objectivity in favor of consternation over the Arendtian idea of 'contempt for facts.' Wells et al. (2019) write,

© KONINKLIJKE BRILL NV, LEIDEN, 2021 | DOI: 10.1163/9789004445376_003

The question for researchers is how, in a so-called 'post-truth' political era when evidence is shunted and emotion is exploited, can we make our research matter to lessen inequality and increase educational opportunities? How do we have an impact when our most conscientious methodology – measuring, understanding, and communicating material and experiential 'realities' – is increasingly discredited by those who construct alternate truths to serve their agendas? (para. 2)

One is tempted to ask here whether there has ever been a 'political era' in which it was it not the case that 'evidence is shunted and emotion is exploited.' But that is, perhaps, beside the point for our present arguments. The leaders of AERA have asserted that the products of modern educational research "measure ... realities" and that such an enterprise is of questionable efficacy because of the era of "post-truth." So, what is their answer to the question of what educational researchers should do in response to the predicament of the products of their research? Wells et al. (2019) state,

We must mobilize interdisciplinary and mixed-method bodies of evidence that coalesce to tell powerful, empirically driven, and multimodal narratives connecting the findings of advanced statistics to the lived experiences of educators, students, and parents across multiple contexts. (para. 4)

In other words, we should produce more of it.

What these leaders of educational research fail to admit is that the very condition they are calling for in the program theme has already arrived in their midst and presently haunts them. The 'democratization of evidence' in everyday life has been assisted by the proliferation of the internet, cable television, satellite radio, podcasts, streaming services, the ubiquity of smartphones and wireless networks, etc. And the democratization of evidence has also already happened in academic research in education not only through some of the same phenomena listed above but also through the proliferation of myriad highly specialized academic journals, open access publishing, the popularity of identity politics research, methodological advances (e.g., autoethnography). One could argue that 'evidence' is more 'democratized' now than ever.

In Baudrillardian terms, this organization has articulated a roadmap to a kind of educational ecstasy (see previous chapter). The call is for more 'evidence,' which necessarily means more information. And the constant proliferation of information, generally, leads to ecstatic forms in which massive amounts of information/data begin to have an inverse effect on what we actually know. The authors of the theme suggest that with more evidence of more different kinds (e.g., 'multimodal'), anti-democratic political forces that hold up progress toward more educational opportunities can be thwarted and the 'contempt for facts' neutralized. But is it really the case that more universal acceptance of the need to 'lessen inequality' will result from the creation of more and different kinds of 'evidence'? Ecstasy in educational research can ultimately only produce a 'radiant and empty form' of educational research.

But perhaps this is a problem of empirical research in education, a problem that philosophy of education avoids? Unfortunately, this is not the case if the problem has something to do with being stuck in traditional modes of critique and thought. A cursory examination of the conference themes and programs of the major organizations in philosophy of education reveals that with few exceptions, the field is committed to traditional forms of critique that Baudrillard was convinced are inefficacious in our current order of simulacra and the contemporary stage of the late capitalist code. However, it is important to point out here that it is not necessarily the objects of the traditional critique in philosophy of education that we think Baudrillard would find wanting. Some of Baudrillard's targets are taken up, broadly speaking, to a significant degree in the field of philosophy of education. However, it is the *form* of critique that Baudrillard rejected that too often still sits at the center of the arguments in the field. In order to more fully understand how Baudrillard's arguments about the end of traditional/dialectical critique might affect philosophy of education or educational research, it is useful to start by getting a sense of his particular ideas of radical thought and in his rise to popularity in the English-speaking world in the 1980s and 1990s. In particular, this starting point helps us make the argument that our current moment is one in which both Baudrillard and his opposition to traditional critique are more useful than ever.

2   The Space for Thinking about Baudrillard

Baudrillard's appearance at the "Chance" event at Whiskey Pete's Casino in 1996 provided a litany of examples of his significant following within the American avant-garde. But that popularity, along with the strident criticisms, seemed to reach its apex around the turn of the 21st century. In terms of academic writing, although his work is demonstrably still a relatively popular choice for a number of lines of theoretical inquiry, the heyday of the most intense and reactionary responses (and at the same time less than 'adequate' or 'convincing' works according to Gane (2000); such as Butler (1999) and Pawlett (2007)) to his ideas and persona are, for the most part, over. It is in this space that it becomes possible to write about Baudrillard, strong evidence of which comes in the form of the founding of the *International Journal of Baudrillard Studies* by the late Gerry Coulter in 2004. Specifically, in educational theory, Trevor Norris (2011) has made an indispensable contribution to Baudrillardian scholarship with "Jean Baudrillard: Consuming Signs," a chapter in his strident critique of consumerism and schooling. When writing about Baudrillard in this relatively new space, it is not as likely to risk association with traditional Marxists who anointed him the "high priest of postmodernism," and declared him a nihilist and a "sign-fetishist" (Norris, 2011, pp. 108–143). Of equal importance to the possibility of writing about Baudrillard is that it is also easier to avoid complicity with the cherry-picking *Matrix* fans and other postmoderns who often employed celebratory misreadings and misapplications of Baudrillard's ideas. Now, after the onslaught of extreme responses to Baudrillard is over, it seems possible to seize the critical distance necessary in order for thought to take place. It is into this space that more satisfying analyses and applications of his work can begin to eclipse the inadequate if not entirely reactionary and cultish responses of the 1980s and 1990s. That is the spirit in which this chapter proceeds. Or, as Baudrillard himself said, "You have to live with the idea that we have survived the worst" (2003, p. 2).

Perhaps 'the worst' in the context of the arguments of this chapter comes in the form of misreadings of Baudrillard in which he was accused of nihilism or of lacking productive value. In order to understand Baudrillard's treatment of traditional critique and to clear the path for his radical thought and fatal theory, it is important to address these misreadings. In other words, if we are to engage his ideas about the inefficacy of dialectical critique, we should also be clear about the productive aspect of this claim and correct the misreadings of his work as exclusively destructive. Particularly, it is fair to say that during the rise of his popularity, Baudrillard's work was misread as nihilistic. Douglas Kellner was convinced of its unequivocal pessimism and stated, "Baudrillard's nihilism is without joy, without energy, without hope for a better future" (Kellner, 1994, p. 12). But Baudrillard himself insisted that fatal theory and radical thought do not lead to despair stating, "[O]ne must fight all charges of irresponsibility, nihilism or despair. Radical thought is never depressive. On this point there is a total misunderstanding" (Baudrillard, 2008, p. 104). In the context of education, there is some amount of hope built in to disabusing ourselves of the notion that dialectical critique has efficacy within the late capitalist code. To continue to commit to what Baudrillard understood as traditional critique is to cling to a modernist project that has no efficacy in the third and fourth orders of simulation (discussed below) and in the late capitalist code. Here we are introducing the Baudrillardian arguments against traditional critique and applying those arguments to critical theoretical work in education that continues its commitment to producing more and more traditional critique. We also introduce Baudrillard's concepts of radical thought and fatal theory as correctives to the dead end of traditional critique, though they will be more fully treated in the last chapter.

3   Baudrillard and Form

Form is an indispensable theme in Baudrillard's writing. As he disposes with traditional or dialectical critique, it must be emphasized that he does not dispense with critique itself. His devastating critiques of the late stages of semiotic culture, simulation, telemorphosis, ecstatic forms, etc., are nearly impossible to miss *qua* critiques. However, his form of critique is non-dialectical and falls outside of traditional critical theoretical approaches. His form is constituted by a novel relationship with the objects of his critique. Gane (2000) put it this way,

> Baudrillard provides not only a theory of the semiotic stages of Western culture, but also a new way of relating to this theory. Thus, as his writings suggest new analyses of simulations, transpolitical forms, virtual cultures, his relation to them is not a critical rationalism. His writing attempts to provoke a paradoxical counter-spiral. And the distance between the two spirals is precisely that of the ritual, the symbolic relation, not one of mastery or possession or *ressentiment*. (p. 21)

The animating idea for this new relation and the concomitant 'paradoxical counter-spiral' that Baudrillard is after in his work is that 'mastery or possession' are impossible in the late capitalist code. That is, the code subsumes every attempt at mastery into its own trajectory. Concerned about alcohol abuse? The large, corporate breweries have it covered as they end their television and radio advertisements with some form of the exhortation to, 'drink responsibly.' Have a critique of gambling culture? Concerned with gambling addiction? So do the online gambling outlets and sports books. Their satellite radio advertisements also end with read-outs of gambling addiction hotline numbers. These are just examples of the myriad ways in which the capitalist code thwarts dialectical critique and the critique of mastery and this is precisely why Baudrillard describes the need for and, indeed, creates a new relationship with the objects of his critique. Again, this is why his emphasis in on form with regard to critique.

4   The Orders of Simulacra

Baudrillard's emphasis on form in critique is a product of his simulation theory and the orders of simulacra. The stability of meaning has changed through orders of simulacra and shifts in the relationship between the sign and the referent. The first order of simulacra is what Baudrillard refers to as The Counterfeit (Pawlett, 2007). It is associated with the beginning of conspicuous consumption and fashion in the sixteenth and seventeenth centuries. In this stage, there becomes a kind of play of arbitrary signs that "have the 'appearance' of being 'bound to the world' but are abstract, referential (re)presentations of it" (Pawlett, 2007, pp. 74–75). The second order is characterized by industrialization and Baudrillard said that the signs characteristic of it are "crude, dull, industrial, repetitive, echoless, functional and efficient" (Baudrillard, 1993, p. 57) whereas signs in the first order "were magical, diabolical, illusory … enchanting" (Pawlett, 2007, p. 76). It is in the third order of simulacra that we get to hyperreality. Here the sign goes through another transformation as representation starts to be replaced by simulation. William Pawlett (2007) puts it this way:

> Simulation is distinct from representation because signifiers lose their attachment to signifieds (the mental 'construction' of meaning inside our heads) as meaning is generated by relations between signifiers ('models') rather than in our reflective or 'inner' dialectical thought processes. Further signs (or rather pre-modelled signifiers) are disarticulated from referents because models *do not have referents*. (p. 76, original emphasis)

Pawlett goes on to use the example of brand names in fashion such as 'Prada' and 'Gucci' to demonstrate that in the third order of simulacra meaning is fully determined by signifiers' relationship to other signifiers. In the first and second orders of simulacra the reality principle remains intact. But in the third order the difference between the real and representation becomes increasingly unstable.

Media today are replete with third order simulacra. When it comes to the image and hyperreality, Baudrillard's reason for lamenting certain aspects of contemporary cinema is this passage into the virtual that Pawlett discusses above (the virtual, for Baudrillard, is totally constitutive of the fourth order of simulacra). In photography the image is two-dimensional and comes closest to a pure image. According to Baudrillard, "It simulates neither time nor movement and confines itself to the most rigorous unreality" (Coulter, 2010, p. 7). On the contrary, with high-definition, enhanced character generation, and so on, that characterize contemporary film and television Zurbrugg (1997) states, "images have passed over into things" and therefore the image "can no longer transcend reality, transfigure it, nor dream it, because it has become its own virtual reality" (p. 12). An illustration of this might be the phenomenon of watching American sporting events on television. It is not uncommon to hear a commentator assert about a particularly spectacular play that a player made 'a video game move' thereby demonstrating the loss of a real world referent. Instead of the video game simulation referring to an actual player, the images of the player in the game on television are signified by the video game. Or, as Baudrillard alludes, the map precedes the territory. That is to say, meaning is generated by relationships between signifiers that have no 'real world' referents. The same can be said for contemporary movies. Coulter (2010) points out the difference between the hyperreal 2006 version of the James Bond film, *Casino Royale* and the original from 1967 by saying that in the former "Bond often has more in common with a video game character than a human actor due to the proliferation of virtual stunts" (p. 16).

5   The Fourth Order and Radical Thought

As Pawlett (2007) rightly points out, Baudrillard scarcely explicitly discussed the fourth order of simulacra in his works.

> Baudrillard's assertions concerning the nature of simulation, specifically the loss of referentiality, make it impossible for him to claim to describe an external 'reality' out there called the fourth order ... Instead Baudrillard developed a number of interrelated themes and notions ... that characterize the fourth order in various ways. (p. 108)

For our purposes, perhaps the most important of these themes that characterize the fourth order is integral or virtual reality. Integral reality becomes possible after 'the murder of the sign' or the complete annihilation of the sign's referentiality. Pawlett (2007) explains, "Without the sign there can be nothing but a virtual copy of the world, a perfected substitute for the world ..." (p. 117). And Baudrillard (2000) said of this,

> By shifting into a virtual world ... We move into a world where everything that exists only as idea, dream, fantasy, will be eradicated, because it will be immediately operationalized ... You will not even have time to imagine ... Everything will be preceded by its virtual realization. (pp. 66–67)

He used contemporary music as one of his examples. Baudrillard (2005) said of 'integral music' that "it can be 'composed' on a computer" and that it "had been clarified and purged, a music restored in its technical perfection. The sound there is not the result of a form; it is actualized by a programme" (Part II). He went on to say,

> the sensorial impact on the listener is also programmed with precision like that of a closed circuit. A virtual music in other words, flawless, deprived of any imagination, mistaken for its own model, the enjoyment of which is also virtual. Is this still music? Nothing is less certain. (Part II)

Given the themes and notions that characterize the fourth order (most notably here integral reality), that is, the full virtualization of the world, critical thought is no longer tenable. In the order of integral reality, the real has fully disappeared and along with it, illusion and the possibility of dialectic critique. One of Baudrillard's later texts, *The Perfect Crime* (2008), discussed the end of critical thought and dismissed it as "intellectually anachronistic" (p. 66) Instead of a world that calls for defending critical values in an as yet unactualized world, Baudrillard described a world in which reality is at its height. This is the world of too much reality and objectivity, not a lack of it, a world of full actualization. Virtuality begets this world in which reality lacks nothing and all negation has been subsumed. And here there is no longer any possibility of critical thought. Baudrillard (2008) said,

> [C]ritical thought ... is in substance ended. Even if it had survived its catastrophic secularization in all the political movements of the twentieth century, this ideal and seemingly necessary relationship between the concept and reality would, at all events, be destroyed today. It has broken down under pressure from a gigantic technical and mental simulation, to be replaced by an autonomy of the virtual, henceforth liberated from the real, and a simultaneous autonomy of the real which we see functioning on its own account in a demented – that is, infinitely self-referential – perspective. (pp. 97–98)

With the onset of the world's virtual double, we have the perfect crime – the murder of the real without a trace of a victim or criminal or motive. But, Baudrillard (2008) also claimed that the perfect crime is actually never quite perfect. This is one reason why fatal theory and radical thought are not depressive.

His critics accused him of nihilism. As we saw above, though, this was a misreading by Marxist scholars who may have had difficulty accepting Baudrillard's post- or non-Marxist critiques. Having described the world as one in which critical thought has ended, he offered radical thought as a more appropriate response to concerns in the third and fourth orders. What is perhaps his most complete description of radical thought also comes from *The Perfect Crime*.

> The other form of thought [radical thought] is eccentric to the real, a stranger to dialectics, a stranger even to critical thought. It is not even a disavowal of the concept of reality. It is illusion, power of illusion, or in other words, a playing with reality, as seduction is a playing with desire, as a metaphor is playing with truth. This radical thought does not stem from a philosophical doubt, a utopian transference, or an ideal transcendence. It is the material illusion, immanent in this so-called 'real' world. (Baudrillard, 2008, p. 97)

Radical thought, then, is able to avoid the pitfalls of critical thought in the third and fourth orders of simulacra. It does not succumb to being subsumed in the way that the negative is subsumed in dialectical critique in the late capitalist code. Instead, it functions on the margins by reincorporating the place of illusion that is lost in the orders of hyperreality and virtuality. Baudrillard claimed, "Radical thought ... anagrammatizes, it disperses concepts and ideas and, by its reversible sequencing, takes account both of meaning and the fundamental illusoriness of meaning" (2008, p. 105). This is the form of thought that we are left with in the world of virtualization.

While much important work has been done using other theoretical orientations, to expose as inefficacious any form of critical or emancipatory theory is constitutive of a Baudrillardian analysis. Again, for our purposes here, this should not be confused as a dismissal of critical thought at the level of motivation or content of concern, but rather as one at the level of theorization and form. For Baudrillard, the late capitalist code is adept at subsuming critique and offering it back as a set of signs to be consumed. The code actually encourages a certain level of critique. What we are left with is fatal theory and fatal strategies, which are ironic strategies that seek to push negative conditions (this is certainly an inadequate description of fatal theory but we return to that subject in the final chapter).

Perhaps a connection to Baudrillard that echoes his ideas above comes from the thesis of Heath and Potter's (2004) book, *Nation of Rebels*. This text's subtitle: *Why Counterculture Became Consumer Culture* approaches the operation of the capitalist code from a sociological and philosophical perspective. Although admittedly these authors fall into the traditional modes of critique and political organization for the solution to the current milieu, it is valuable to connect their diagnosis of the reason counterculture was absorbed by the capitalist code with Baudrillard's description of the late capitalist code expressed above.

In short, the argument for Heath and Potter is that counter to the story of the 1960's counterculture tells itself, was not revolutionary, or rebellious – it actually worked hard in implicit, and now looking back with our 21st century eyes, explicit ways to perform the opposite of its professed goals to bring down society. As referenced in the Introduction, the television show Mad Men with the Coke ad's appropriation of the hippie movement themes to sell its drink, instead of 'sticking it to the man' these movements actually re-enforced capitalism mechanisms by changing the function of its signs. Thus, Coke instead of being the drink for the regular people, was now the choice of the peace-loving hippie. This demonstrates the functionality of the sign in which its chameleonic nature is now the default setting. Advertising proliferates into today's version, where a way for Coke to be drunk by any subgroup or counterculture and this operation of late capitalism becomes the point of order for everything.

The thesis of the *Nation of Rebels* becomes clear in a set of case studies revealing that the counterculture was actually more capitalistic that the previous order, and was not able to effectively combat the negative effects of capitalism given their set of misguided assumptions about how change occurs. As Heath and Potter (2004) state, "Having fun is not subversive, and it doesn't undermine any system" (p. 9). There is no dropping out of capitalism. In fact, having fun becomes capitalistic, or all of our time and space it operationalized in advance by capitalism, or the current functioning of the simulacrum.

Counterculture, pop culture, subcultures simply created more opportunities for capitalist code to subsume culture within its practices. As culture proliferated into 'rebel' or sub genres, the capitalist code was dynamic and like the algorithms of today's code (more in next few chapters) simply incorporated the 1960s counter culture, and every iteration of its 'rejection' of norms within its grasp. In fact, the authors' claim that the most revolutionary force to change society has actually been the capitalist code itself. Unfortunately, the authors fail to take up the radical thought offered by Jean Baudrillard. But we think their diagnosis of the effectiveness of capitalism is another way to wade into the issues of the failure of traditional critique to change society.

6   Radical Thought in Practice: Baudrillard's Theory-Fiction

Baudrillard left us with more than just descriptions and analysis of the concept of radical thought. In his later work, he provided examples of it in his writing. Beginning in the mid-1980s, his writing becomes increasingly aphoristic,

poetic, polemic, and hyperbolic – all methods and styles that remain effica-
cious after the end of dialectic critique. The travelogue/journal series, *Cool
Memories I–V* (1990–2004) is paradigmatic of this. Yet, as Gane (2000) has
noted, throughout this stylistic commitment Baudrillard was "undoubtedly
profoundly systematic and even highly rationalistic" (p. 21). In other words, the
paradox of Baudrillard's late writing is that it both avoids the inefficacy of a
particular set of rationalistic *styles of critique* while remaining systematic and
rationalistic. He achieves this through form. Unlike the conventional theorist
who attempts to master her or his object, the fatal theorist seeks to anticipate
the irony of the object. "If the world is paradoxical, theory must be even more
paradoxical" (Gane, 2000, p. 21).

   Coulter (2007b) pointed out that Baudrillard's "writing is one of the delight-
ful examples of the way in which theory and literature begin to communicate
with such affection in the late 20th century (when theory finally accepted
itself as fiction)" (Part II). To misunderstand Baudrillard as lacking seriousness
as a theorist is to misunderstand his entire project. Theory and fiction come
together, out of necessity for Baudrillard, in a world in which dialectical critique has become intellectually anachronistic. In this world, critical theory and
critical thought are subsumed back into the capitalist code and repurposed as
sets of signs to be consumed alongside the rest in the steady waltz of images
without referents that is constitutive of our telemorphic trajectory. As Pawlett
(2007) has pointed out, this is precisely why Che Guevara T-shirts exist. Coulter
understood this as well. Coulter authored the most precise and memorable
sobriquet for Baudrillard's *Cool Memories* series when he called them, "theory
diaries" (2007a, Part II). As the title of his review of *Cool Memories V*, Coulter
used one of the more revealing quotes in the book, and one that gets directly
into the heart of Baudrillard's late work, "Theory is never so fine as when it
takes the form of a fiction or a fable" (2007a).

   Baudrillard advocated, explicitly and by example in his late writings, a kind
of serious playing with theory, fiction, and myth. This kind of play has perhaps never had more socio-political use than it does in our current landscape
(and as Coulter, 2007b, has taught us, "Writing *was* Baudrillard's politics"). In
response to the political phenomena of Brexit, Trump, Le Pen and the concomitant ubiquity of concerns over 'fake news' and 'information wars' significant numbers on the Left have championed a commitment to 'The Truth' and
'Objectivity' but these all fall under a form of response that was already, in Baudrillard's view, anachronistic in the 1980s. Theory-fiction/fable (playing with
meaning) is the only way to avoid the trap of our critiques being subsumed
into the code.

It is this theory-fiction or, radical thought in practice that the world after dialectical critique, after critical theory, after the third (and perhaps fourth) order of simulacra calls for. Indeed, in a world in which 'the dialectic is definitively over' theory must be put into conversation with fiction and myth (and diaries). Baudrillard (2008) said we must "Promote a clandestine trade in ideas, of all inadmissible ideas, of unassailable ideas, as the liquor trade had to be promoted in the 1930s. For we are already in a state of full-scale prohibition" (p. 66).

7   Conclusion

More discussion of radical thought, theory-fiction and their connection to fatal theory follows in the final chapter of this book. At the conclusion of this chapter, we return to the ecstatic forms of education that are produced from the doubling down on the role of critical and dialectal thought in education and in philosophy of education. Baudrillard said that ecstatic forms were 'pure and empty' and that is precisely what we make of what results from the reliance on critical thought and dialectical forms of critique in educational research broadly and in philosophy of education specifically. There is a direct relationship between the overproduction of information in education (or what the American Educational Research Association has recently called 'multimodal narratives' that produce the 'democratization of evidence') and the way in which the academic products of those in the field of philosophy of education rely on dialectical critique. That is, the commitment to critical thought leads to overproduction of information and ecstatic forms because critical thought is subsumed by the code, the negative of the dialectic is swallowed up and repurposed by the code and all that is left for those committed to dialectical critique is to produce more of it.

References

Baudrillard, J. (1990). *Cool memories*. Verso Books.

Baudrillard, J. (1993). *Symbolic exchange and death*. Sage Publications.

Baudrillard, J. (1996). *Cool memories II, 1987–1990* (C. Turner, Trans.). Duke University Press.

Baudrillard, J. (1997). *Fragments: Cool memories III, 1990–1995*. Verso Books.

Baudrillard, J. (2000). *The vital illusion*. Columbia University Press.

Baudrillard, J. (2003). *Cool memories IV: 1995–2000*. Verso Books.

Baudrillard, J. (2005). Violence of the virtual and integral reality. *International Journal of Baudrillard Studies, 2*(2). https://baudrillardstudies.ubishops.ca/violence-of-the-virtual-and-integral-reality/

Baudrillard, J. (2006). *Cool memories V: 2000–2004* (C. Turner, Trans.). Polity.

Baudrillard, J. (2008). *The perfect crime.* Verso Books.

Butler, R. (1999). *Jean Baudrillard: The defence of the real.* Sage Publications.

Coulter, G. (2007a). Theory is never so fine as when it takes the form of a fiction or fable. *International Journal of Baudrillard Studies, 4*(2).

Coulter, G. (2007b). Jean Baudrillard's writing about writing. *International Journal of Baudrillard Studies, 4*(3). https://baudrillardstudies.ubishops.ca/jean-baudrillards-writing-about-writing/

Coulter, G. (2010). Jean Baudrillard and cinema. The problems of technology, realism and history. *Film Philosophy, 14*(2), 6–20.

Gane, M. (2000). *Jean Baudrillard: In radical uncertainty.* Pluto Press.

Heath, J., & Potter, A. (2004). *Nation of rebels.* Harper Collins.

Kellner, D. (1994). *Baudrillard: A critical reader.* Blackwell.

Norris, T. (2011). *Consuming schools: Commercialism and the end of politics.* University of Toronto Press.

Pawlett, W. (2007). *Jean Baudrillard: Against banality* (Vol. 12). Taylor & Francis.

Wells, A. S., Jellison Holme, J., & Scott, J. T. (2019). *Leveraging education research in a "post-truth" era: Multimodal narratives to democratize evidence.* AERA 2019 Conference Opening. https://www.aera.net/Portals/38/2019%20Theme_FINAL.pdf

Zurbrugg, N. (1997). *Jean Baudrillard, art and artefact.* Sage Publications.

CHAPTER 3

From Representation to Simulation

1 Introduction: *The Reality We Have 'Now'* ...

> The third doctrine is that Life imitates Art far more than Art imitates Life.
> (Oscar Wilde, 1891)

This quotation is taken from Oscar Wilde's work *The Decay of Lying: An Observation* from 1891. He created the text in the vein of a Socratic dialogue in which characters named after his children, Cyril and Vivian, debate many things, most importantly to us here, the notion of facts, social reality, and representation. There are two conclusions in this work that are clairvoyant in regards to Jean Baudrillard's concepts. The first is the quotation above, that 'life' imitates 'art' – not the other way around. In other words, the realities we create, the worlds we imagine, the spaces humans make, these 'arts,' are then the template for life. In Baudrillardian speak: the map (art) precedes the territory (life). The reversal of the reality function in Wilde and Baudrillard, of what we normally construct as the flowing of artistic formations as an imitation (memesis) of life, makes simulation and simulacra as a description of this opposite reality function an important phenomenon to study.

As Baudrillard (1981/1994) states, "The territory no longer precedes the map, nor does it survive it" (p. 1). Thus life, in our late modern era, is more and more imitated and it follows, or is coded by 'art.' Baudrillard, in the quote above, adds the clause "nor does it survive it." This links to the second point from Wilde's dialogue that lying, not fact, is the highest aim of art. Art at its core is simulacra following all the way back to Plato. For Wilde and to some degree Baudrillard, lying, telling beautiful untruths (simulation), is actually what creates reality; and furthermore, it destroys reality as any direct 'correspondence' to truth being objectively connected to the world.[1] Deeper still, and to Wilde's point (and perhaps for us, to fatal theory), is that truth does not survive lying, especially when it is beautiful. The simulation of the simulacra is an aesthetic action.[2] This aesthetic dimension activates political spaces with which we find ourselves all too familiar. This is another aspect of what we have previously described as Badurillardian spaces in Chapter 1.

These tensions of reality, truth, simulacra, beauty, etc., create a deterrence or a feeling of unease within the world. This 'unease' is where we will examine the ideas of Baudrillard with a focus on his deployment of the concepts of

© KONINKLIJKE BRILL NV, LEIDEN, 2021 | DOI: 10.1163/9789004445376_004

simulacra and simulation. This chapter will contend that Baudrillard's concept of simulation in particular, has a bearing on, and creates an implicit imperative on everyday experience. In fact, simulation is always already 'undergone.' We must not shy away from Baudrillard's warning that all of human life is heading towards total encoding by the logic of simulation and that this 'reality' we have 'now' will not endure. No reality can ever endure as simulation does not function with a reality principle based on representation.

Before we get to the logic of simulation today, let us return to Wilde's time, for this is perhaps one of many possible beginning trajectories of simulation and helps begin to reveal Baudrillard's ideas. Given the Victorian mores and the context of Wilde's essay, he was after a description in some sense of the ways in which social situations, the social conduct of the day, the way humans created 'reality' was via lying. Or perhaps the 'decorum' of the Victorian life was simply to live a 'lie.' The way a gentleman should act, and in his case, a hetero-normative structure in which Wilde was literally held to legally (and was eventually prosecuted for violating), was the fundamental lie of the day. The reality they had 'then' was structured, simulated via these lies, and we find in Wilde an inversion of the function of truth (representation of reality) into a description of truth where reality follows art.

This particular lesson from the Victorian era is clear, and for our purposes generalizable– human societies create systems that rely on lies that feed into norms and culture. These simulacra are simulated as functional actions that are taken as default settings for reality. In creating *systems of reality* (maps or 'art') that *ex post facto* becomes *reality* (the territory or 'life'), humans have culture through representation of these 'lies.' Thus, for the Victorian, society and human experience was supposed to represent the values of their day, and was 'performed' or re-presented in signs à al culture, just as our norms are based on lies of our day. Baudrillard examined situations like these closely, and was determined to established simulation over representation as the logic of experience and culture. Let us now examine this shift from representation to simulation more closely.

2   From Representation to a *Hyperspace without Atmosphere*

Reality itself then, like Baudrillard (1981/1994) said in his essay the *Precession of the Simulacra*, is ruled by rules (codes), maps, mores, etc. To illustrate the point, Baudrillard evokes the Borges fable of an emperor requesting the map of his empire which through a series of presentations and inaccuracies by the map makers, leads to the most accurate map being the empire itself. The best

map of the empire, the most precise representation, is the one you are stand-
ing on. The lesson here being that any representation of reality is conditional.
It relies on signs, or a context connected to the real world (re-presentation of
objective material reality). Better yet, representation always relies on signs
conditioned with the 'arts' at hand, and in the contexts of the day (Victorian
signs for a Victorian reality) that can best 'reproduce' the real world. So, in each
context there are different ways the objective material world was represented
by contextual signs. As representation becomes ever more 'accurate' (with better tools or 'arts'), it leads to its own demise, the map makers will eventually
'walk on the map,' causing the need for particular types of representation to
disappear.

Put another way, the reality we have now is not the reality of the Victorian
era as the context has changed. Victorian reality had a code, a set of unspoken
implicit 'rules' which reality was 'enforced.' Experiencing things outside of this
'code' was deviant from reality, or literally 'un-real.' The implicit forces shaping
reality (signs) are the roots of reality, and if a person was 'out of code' then they
were in a sense 'out of reality.' Homosexuality, which is normal and 'happens'
all the time was not conceivable – or not conceivable as the desired reality of
the Victorian context. But signs change through the ages. They expand their
meaning fields, different operations for reality form, and new coding is inevi-
tably developed.

However, Baudrillard made the point that the reality we have now is not only
coded differently because of context shifting, but coded differently because
the mechanism for 'forming' reality has shifted from representation to simulation.
"This imaginary of representation, which simultaneously culminates in and is
engulfed by the cartographer's mad project of the ideal coextensivity of map
and territory, disappears in the simulation ..." (Baudrillard, 1981/1994, p. 2). For
Baudrillard, representation – or a reality that corresponded directly to objects
has been eclipsed not only by new contexts and new signs, but by a new way
of forming reality altogether. The real world has shifted into a more intensive
coding and production operation.

> No more mirror of being and appearances, of the real and its concept.
> No more imaginary coextensivity: it is genetic miniaturization that is the
> dimension of simulation. The real is produced from miniaturized cells,
> matrices, and memory banks, models of control – and it can be reproduced
> an indefinite number of times from these. (Baudrillard, 1981/1994, p. 2)

Reality as simulation is 'operational' or what Baudrillard called 'hyperreal.'
What this means is that in Baudrillard's view the real had shifted from being

produced through representational mechanisms, which mirrored the objects and world around us to being simulated – or in simulation. "... simulation corresponds to a corruption of reality through signs; simulation corresponds to a short circuit of reality and to its duplication through signs" (Baudrillard, 1981/1994, p. 27). Simulation is a procession or better yet a '*circulation*' in which reality decouples with any sense that the objective world truly matters and/or creates the reality we have now. In a sense art, as symbolic circulation of models of the real for the real (simulacra), has literally become the stuff of life.

Another way to rethink 'reality' creation is that representation was the way in which we tried to stop the circulation of reality whereas simulation 'lubricates' reality – lets it move in an out/in, up and down – without origins or the need for them. In other words, reality and representation need to correspond to something, an original 'copy,' a re-presentation of the material world. Simulation drops that correlation. Instead we are walking around on the map grasping for clues to that point us back to a representation of a territory (the map) that has disappeared. This shift to simulation is admittedly hard to understand given our culture's empirical inclinations. To help explain the phenomena, Baudrillard creates a narrative that reveals his thoughts on the shift to simulation from representation. This shift is key to his thinking and understanding the importance of his theory's contribution to philosophy.

At this point one might object – what is wrong with reality? Or what is wrong with the idea the reality is a representation of an objective material world? Isn't that so? Why did Baudrillard think this representational model has changed or is no longer valid in the current context? Much like the critiques of the correspondence theory of truth, in which truths built by corresponding truth to 'reality' of the 'real' world is questioned, Baudrillard saw evidence that that this 'representational theory of truth' had disappeared in simulation's circulation – which radiates in every direction – (as opposed to a 'one way' representational objective world to its sign linear relationship). Baudrillard (1981/1994) states, "... it is no longer a question of either maps or territories. Something has disappeared: the sovereign difference, between one and the other, that constituted the charm of abstraction" (p. 2) The charm of abstraction, the notion that we have an objective world that we abstract, represent, and perfectly code as reality no longer works in the circulation of simulation. According to Baudrillard,

> It is no longer a question of imitation, nor duplication, nor even parody. It is a question of substituting the signs of the real for the real, that is to say of an operation of deterring every real process via its operational double,

a programmatic, metastable, perfectly descriptive machine that offers all the signs of the real and short-circuits all its vicissitudes. Never again will the real have the chance to produce itself .... (1981/1994, p. 2)

Simulation not only replaces representation, it prevents representational logic from re-forming or coming back into circulation. Representation disappears for good in the logic of simulation.

This is the narrative Baudrillard was working hard to establish as his simulation theory. Simulation asphyxiates representational thinking and creates a predatory logic of the simulation. This logic is as follows: the principle of reality itself is antiquated. The correspondence theories of truth, and representational reality [epistemology, metaphysics, "It is all of metaphysics that is lost" (Baudrillard, 1981/1994, p. 2)] in general that rely on the 'classic sign system' in which signs referred to an object in the world (an original referent) is no longer functioning in this way. The map makers, once presenting the map as empire itself, have let the genie out of the bottle.

Additionally, Baudrillard's narrative considers that as the 20th century created ever more systems or models of simulation that integrated deeper into the human experience, these modes of living have failed to re-create a representational reality. In his earlier work, Baudrillard submitted that symbolic value (over use-value, exchange value) made the sign as signifier most important – or containing more value – or was more real than the sign's objective connection to the world (the referent). In his logic the signifying value replaces both exchange value and use value – thus cancelling out the object relations (representation) of the sign; the sign, in the reality we have now, is purely symbolic. Thus, the object reference has disappeared. That is, the 'real' world as we had previously constituted it has disappeared. Simulation has swallowed up representation's ability to form a 'reality that matters.' Simulation is a 'predator of reality' as previously philosophized. Here is Baudrillard's wording: "Whereas representation attempts to absorb simulation by interpreting it as a false representation, simulation envelops the whole edifice of representation as itself a simulacrum" (1981/1994, p. 6). This is Baudrillard's logic, the new reality principle – simulation is running amok.

3   The Entangled Orders of Simulacra: *Disneyland, Disneyworld, Disneyverse*

Disneyland is a perfect model for all the entangled orders of the simulacra. (Baudrillard, 1981/1994, p. 12)

It is rumored that Theodore Adorno called Walt Disney the most dangerous man in America (Delanty, 2004). In terms of impact and popular culture the role Disney plays in the United States and globally cannot be overestimated. At minimum it affects the culture on many levels, and for Baudrillard serves as a perfect example for explaining his ideas of simulacra and simulation further.

As explained above, Baudrillard's orders of simulacrum is for him a logic in which simulation has replaced representation as the functioning mechanization of reality. There are four 'entangled' orders of simulacra, as outlined in the previous chapter. Here we explain these orders further and in the context of the 'perfect model,' Disney. In *the first order of simulacra*, the representation of the real is direct. We are not in the least bit fooled by the 'lie.' It is *the second order simulacra* that begins to blur the boundary of reality and representation. This is the 'discrete charm' of the map in Borges fable story alluded to earlier in this chapter and in the previous chapter. To recap, the second order of simulacra confuses the real and representation so that one cannot always tell the difference. The 'map can be the territory.' The representation of the real is as real as the real. It is the *third order of simulacra* that we find ourselves eclipsed by in contemporary everyday life. Here the simulacra precede reality, or better put, the circulation of simulacra replaces a reality based on representation, as mentioned in the previous section. Added later by Baudrillard (2009), but not fully developed in his work, the *fourth order of simulacra*,[3] would be truly 'fractal' in the sense all values are yet to come, or deferred and multiplied as one examines them (like a fractal in geometry); much like the post-truth and post-political mechanisms that are experienced more and more today.

Although the orders of simulacrum were briefly described in the last chapter in the context of the end of traditional critique, here we discuss them further in the specific context of Baudrillard's simulation theory. In order to do this, we use the same example Baudrillard uses – Disney. However, since the late 1970's when Baudrillard wrote about Disney, the sophistication and manipulation of 'reality' Disney has embarked upon has not in the least lessened his ideas, but terrifyingly deepened them (especially concerning the incoming fourth, fractal order). Let's start with a recap of Baudrillard's (1981/1994) use of Disney in his text '*the Precession of Simulacra*' from the early 1980's.

3.1   *Disneyland – The Third Order Simulation*

Walt Disney wanted to create the ideal park, one in which families would be presented, like a Potemkin village, with an illusion of a reality that would represent his ideals for the American experience. Families would come to the park and escape 'reality' by being inundated, or presented with another one – what

FIGURE 3   Brandenburger Strasse, Potsdam, Germany

FIGURE 4   Main Street, Over-the-Rhine, Cincinnati, OH

Baudrillard has called hyperreality. Disneyland was to be a mix of nostalgia and deterrence established when they plowed under an orange grove in Anaheim California in 1954. As Baudrillard (1981/1994) remarked: "When the real is no longer what it was, nostalgia assumes its full meaning" (p. 6). Disneyland would contain a hyper-sense of nostalgia, for an American main street that was gone, for an American ideal that was in danger of being eclipsed. In fact, the 'Mainstreet USA' was a key element in the Disneyland (and shortly thereafter, Disneyworld) theme parks. Let's examine some visual examples that help connect what Baudrillard was trying to relay.

In Figures 3 and 4 we have images of main streets. The first, Figure 3, is Brandenburger Strasse in Potsdam, Germany. It is a baroque main street that was in a sense 'copied' in the second image, Figure 4, of the Over-the-Rhine districts main street in Cincinnati, Ohio created in the nineteenth century and pictured here today. This second street, Figure 4, updated the Baroque facades but in essence is the same 'code' for main street. By the time Walt Disney was creating Disneyland in the 1950's, this notion of main street was at its apex. Ideally American main streets were places where one would feel at home and relax in the order of business and in conducting a way of life. Only a few decades later, as the American de-industrialization by corporations and political policies devastated main streets across America, would this ideal physically fade away. This physical rotting of our notion of the main street left the ideal Disney projected in the 1950's as a leftover sign untethered to physical realities of American streets across the country. American main street lost its physical origin (there are fewer and fewer actual main streets such as these functioning), and got replaced by a symbolic one. If one searches for images of main street at Disneyland (past and present) they will be confronted with eerie similarities to the pictures shown in Figures 3 and 4. Ironically, yet as Baudrillard's thinking will explain, main street Disneyland is an ideal that today is frequently absent from a lot of American experiences in their own communities. The American main street reality has disappeared. In fact, as we reengineered our communities into suburban geographies, we chose to build main streets as malls as opposed to actual main streets (Hardwick, 2004). As the Disney corporation grew and expanded to Florida, it built Disneyworld's main street in 1971, which upped the ante of this nostalgic exercise by putting a castle at the end of the road (we will discuss Disneyworld shortly).

When walking down main street in Disneyland, one gets the sense of a deterrent moment, a feeling of deterrence (see the introduction of this book for a review). For Baudrillard deterrence is an important aspect of the everyday life of the simulation. For him Disneyland is a 'deterrence machine' in which we experience fantasy as reality, or a nostalgia that longs for a reality we just might seek to create once outside the park itself, even if it is physically impossible (given the conditions of actual main streets in deindustrialized U.S. cities). This deterrence experience essentially sets up the situation in which the simulation of the real is the functional operation of reality. We seek in Disney an indulgence in the fantasy that there was a real world of American main streets, and we enter the park with a feeling of deterrence that our idea of an ideal outside world can be experienced without actually having to go to 'real places' – because Disneyland stands in for all places as the function of simulation replaces reality itself. In the experience of Disneyland, we begin to resent our outside world as being too real – in which poverty, funk, drugs and grime, all of which Disney seeks to hide, would interrupt reality as it now functions in simulation. In our simulation age, we now seek out and prefer the lie to the 'truth.' We prefer the ideal (aesthetic) simulation of Disneyland's main streets to the unsightly realism main streets contain.

As Baudrillard notes:

> Disneyland exists in order to hide that it is the 'real' country, all of 'real' America that *is* Disneyland ... Disneyland is presented as imaginary in order to make us believe that the rest is real .... (1981/1994, p. 12)

In other words, Disneyland as an experience is simulation – neither real nor false – but a place where we in a sense disorient ourselves, and begin to seek real experiences as a tourist, visitor, consumer or main street shopper all the time. With simulation we now think Disney's main street is the real and 'real main streets' in our own towns should change and conform to this ideal simulation. It doesn't matter that this authentic family experience is completely artificial – so is most of modern life. We are always already tourists everywhere now that simulation is the order of everyday life. Baudrillard goes on: "... whereas all of Los Angeles and the America that surrounds it [Disneyland] are no longer real, but belong to the hyperreal order and to the order of simulation" (1981/1994, p. 12). The hyperreal order has bled out of Disneyland and into the entire terraformed planet. Every city, every space, every main street in a sense is now Disneyland. This Baudrillardian space always creates our experiences as 'tourism.' That *is* the code for authentic living in our age. This is further explained in Disneyworld's creation.

3.2   *Disneyworld – The Third Order, Simulation's Simulation*
Frankly speaking, Disneyworld is a simulation of Disneyland. In 1971, a few years after Walt Disney died, Disneyworld opened in a terraformed drained swamp outside Orlando Florida. This second iteration took lessons and expanded upon the Disneyland park and focused not only on creating an American ideal, but seemingly a global or world simulation machine. There was of course more land to alter, more money, more ideas, and more to do.

On the surface Disneyworld's Main Street is an important hub of the park, but, like the suburban expansion of America itself, it is actually simply a walk

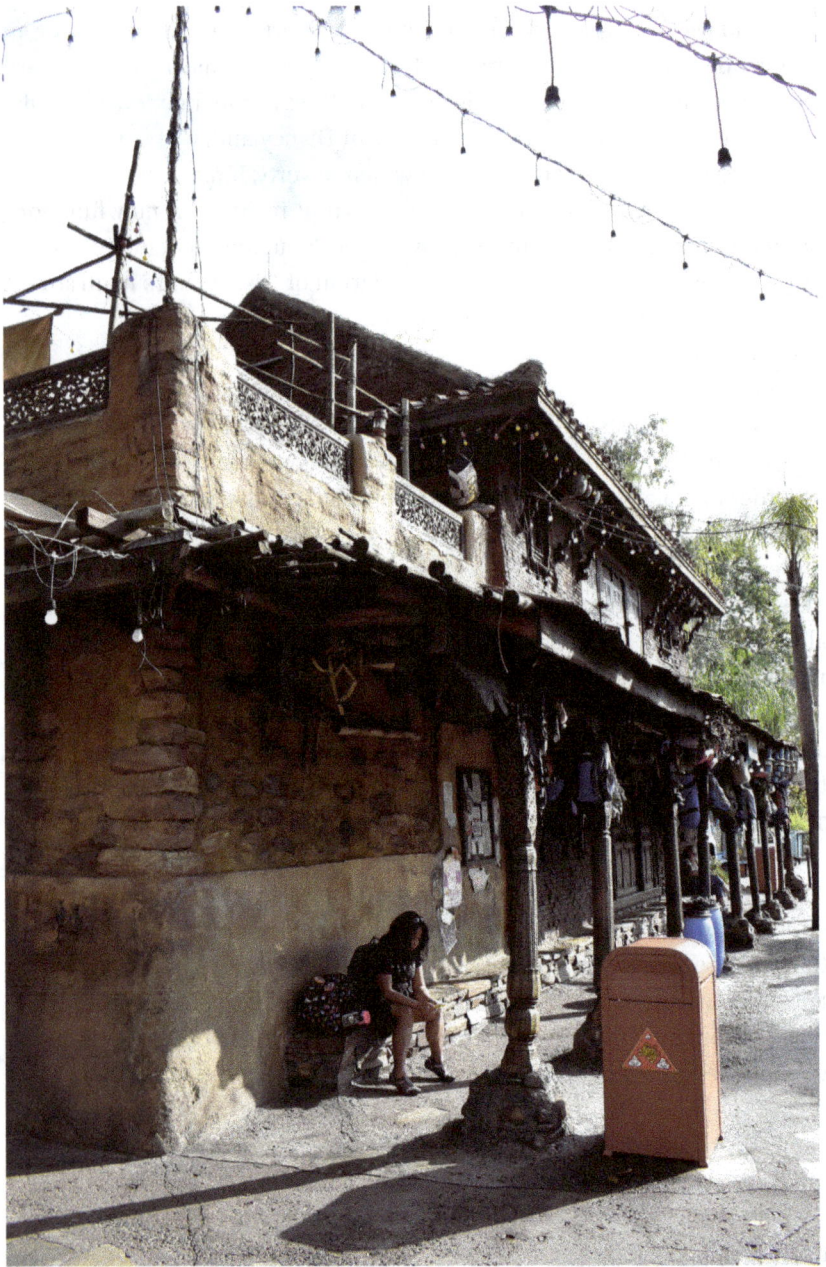

FIGURE 5 Animal Kingdom
PHOTOGRAPH: © KRISTOPHER HOLLAND, DISNEYWORLD THEME PARK

through (drive through) to other parks or spaces – it is a gateway to the 'world.'
Importantly, Walt Disney's vision for the park which was not fully realized
until after his death (the Experimental Prototype Community of Tomorrow –

EPCOT – was to be a whole simulated ideal American community). Disney-world was created not only to present people with a nostalgic main street, but a living model of the future involving a whole community. It was to truly 'map the territory' of America's future, and would give the tourist code (reality) a further spin – as the park experience actually strives to simulate the simulation of the American ideal life colonized to the world. This 'world' would not simply consume the time of a weekend trip at an amusement park, but instead simulate or encode the whole life of the visitor, or tenants of the park when they are there. It would expand the Disney operation to get you not only to think their main street was the 'real' one and yours must change to fit this program, but that other parts of the world are also in need of Disney-fication. To that end, in the decades since the park has opened it has been augmented in order to fine tune the simulation into 'non-American' places.

The photographs in Figures 5–7 are taken from the extension to the 1971 park plan build called Animal Kingdom. This experience features villages from Africa, the Himalayas and a large 'tree of life.' The sophistication of the 'total immersion' experience is important here. Notice from Figures 5, 6 and 7 even the 'spaghetti electrical lines' and damaged or degraded architecture is recreated. Thus, American imperialism is encoded and the ideal for Africa is presented as shabby power lines and dilapidated buildings. The simulation of Africa sees this imperfect state as its ideal, and one can imagine an American then visiting African countries expecting to see those things, much like our main streets are expected to look like Disney's.

What is insidious about simulation is that everyone knows they are in a fake village, but the point is not to fool you into thinking you are in the African context, but to prove the ability of the Disney company to simulate, whatever the terrain, whatever the place, *any* place as ideal. Disney wants to simulate Africa in the abstraction to stimulate an experience which we will internalize and continually project and expect, not represent it authentically or originally. The whole park is a flexing of the muscle of Disney's simulation abilities to re-create anything. This is 'maps proceeding territories,' and the idea that if we want to, art can create life – an experience of the African village in the ideal sense – without the messy fact of actually being in Africa. We could, if we wanted to, do this (create an African village) anywhere – and this is the real point – we have the ability to create any reality, of any human built environment, almost anywhere at any time (given the money etc.). One can imagine a Disneyverse in the future where each town or even home has elements or simulation power of any reality they want (if that isn't what suburban American is, as an idea, already). The code is now digital and machines can simply make the themes of the park come to you. We can all have Disneyworlds not just in our minds after visiting the park, but in our own homes.[4]

FIGURE 6   Animal Kingdom, African village
PHOTOGRAPH: © KRISTOPHER HOLLAND, DISNEYWORLD THEME PARK

FIGURE 7   Animal Kingdom, Himalaya
PHOTOGRAPH: © KRISTOPHER HOLLAND, DISNEYWORLD THEME PARK

3.3   *The Disneyverse – Fourth Order Simulation – The Emergent Fractal Simulation*

This ability to simulate at will is reflected in what we might call, for our purposes here, the *Disneyverse*. The Disneyverse is, in our sense of the term, the precedence of simulation over everything that is real to the point of total immersion. The Disney corporation is a media conglomerate that has the ability to completely surround a person with its products in the home, or better yet 'its reality.' The architecture of persuasion advertising companies use to get people to buy their products has been mastered by Disney with its 'youth outreach' (aka. movies, toys, cartoons, etc.), and control of leisure time (and time in general). Again, the Disneyverse is not just the parks and media products but more importantly the ideals, the ideologies it creates which are now accessible to everyone around the clock and around the world. In essence, there is a Disney cultural algorithm that is used to 'Disney-fy' the simulation function. This hijacking in turn creates the Disneyverse, which is like a fractal expansion of Disney itself.

The Disneyverse example is the seed of the fourth order of simulacrum – the fractal order. In the fourth order, the idea of truth itself is no longer a condition for reality, and the idea of truth itself is similar to the notion of post-truth so popular in politics today. A fractal creates a never-ending process of delaying reality – or reality is postponed forever as one looks closer at it, all they see is more of the same. This is the simulation of the fourth order. Disney not only seeks to be the code of our realities, but to dominate the coding process by also creating the *place* it can happen – your experiences – your 'reality' – your thoughts, etc. are all done on Disney's terms, in a way. For example, if you are a young creative person and want to work on films, etc., Disney's formula, or code is an option, which the company deeply dreams of making the only option. Disney does this even, legally, as in 1996 when the United States Congress changed copyright law (Telecommunications Act of 1996, 1996). In short, the idea here is that Disney wants to create the illusion that there is no outside to their ability to 'imagineer' our realities. In a sense, the worlds they control are not only the engineering of a park, or the intellectual properties, entertainment, etc., but creating the expectation that someday reality itself will be the Disneyverse. Baudrillard's example of Disney from the early 1980s has only multiplied into a deeper exemplar for his ideas about everyday life in the contemporary condition of simulation to which we now turn.

4   The Precession of Simulation: The Decay/Delay/Displacement of Reality

In a sense the Disneyverse seeks to make living into perpetually being a tourist of Disney's presentations of things, music, film, parks, T.V., etc.; but Disney is simply a straw-person, or has until now 'held the place' for the precession of simulation as everyday life. For Baudrillard this is how we experience the world now. What is the precession of simulation? Baudrillard (1981/1994) gives us some insight: "... we are in a logic of simulation, which no longer has anything to do with a logic of facts and an order of reason. Simulation is characterized by a *precession of the model*" (p. 16). Understanding what he means by models is important. Models are systems, logics, maps, objects, etc. of reality that we mistake for reality itself. "... the models come first, their circulation, orbital like that of the bomb, constitutes the genuine magnetic field of the event" (p. 16). Implicit in the encounter with the simulation, or events, is that models are precursors to what we experience as reality – they are the precession, the preceding act, the precedence. In a sense we always have models of reality neuroscientifically,[5] but for Baudrillard they are the point and possibility of simulation's circulation. The notion of 'the market' in economics at the heart of the neoliberal ideology, the 'magical thinking' of Christianity [see Hedges (2006, 2009) to explore this notion more], the 'political unicorns' of the post-truth American politics, game theory's notion of human nature, behaviorism's notions of how we learn, Freudian psychology, etc., these are all models we mistake for reality. These are all models as precession that we come to experience via the function of simulation – our lives imitating art.

Thus, we are all encountering the simulation as events of life, which privileges models. Baudrillard is simply pointing to how reality is created and experienced via these precedence – models. Most important, he is also warning us – not encouraging this simulation's procession into the fourth order, but aiming to figure out its structure in order to formulate a strategy (fatal strategies) to resist this impending logic. This warning against fractal reality must permeate all aspects of life because going down that path leads to dangerous functions or models that will make reality – dangerous dark arts will create life. As Baudrillard (1981/1994) states: "Simulation is infinitely more dangerous because it always leaves open to supposition that, above and beyond its object, *law and order themselves might be nothing but simulation*" (p. 20). One of the potential consequences of the future of simulation is not only that is does not function like previous orders simulacrum, but the unraveling of our ability to have any notion of things like justice will be lost in a functional way. The simulation in the third order will give way to functions not only outside the binary of true and false, but inaugurate a new age of fractal simulation where the possibilities to recover communication, truth, self, other, etc., will also disappear. Here we share a few short examples that commence trajectories to the fourth order horizon approaching our everyday lives.

5   The Case of *Salvator Mundi* and Atomic Printed *Mona Lisa*

The $450 million Leonardo da Vinci painting called *Salvator Mundi*'s prove-
nance has been in question for some time (Jones, 2018). However, it is presently authenticated enough to command the price and is labeled as a 'da Vinci.'
What is important about this 'case' can be used to illustrate Baudrillard's warning about simulation. As an example of simulation, the fact that the *Salva-
tor Mundi* is authentically a da Vinci painting doesn't actually matter. What
matters is the simulation of its reality is believed, or its simulated existence
triggers in the human mind enough of a 'reality' to place it into a circulation
of images (or signs for 'da Vinci') and hence circulate that da Vinci sign – eventually the circulation of the sign becomes reality itself (or the painting never
has to be authentic, because the sign is). It doesn't matter if it was ever real as
long the operation that makes things real is real. What counts is that the operation of reality – simulation – is what we now count on as making the real. The
frightening future is that when gazing into this reality machine (simulation not
representation) all we see is more and more reality (a la fractals). In that movement all we ever see is more precession of simulacra, more models edging us
closer to the fourth order simulacra.

Given this, once we have the technology in the future to electronically (or
atomically) scan and print 'objects,' we will then be able to place them anywhere.
Put another way, we might be able to fractalize any object (creating infinite
copies for infinite contexts). The *Mona Lisa* (or its electron level scanned and
'printed' version) can be on your mantel – Duchamp's urinal can be in your living
room. This is infinitely 'better' than that Van Gogh poster in your dorm room – as
it is literally, at the atomic level, the same object or thing. In a fourth order simulation, the ability to make reality as these printed atomic level objects is only
part of the point. Ultimately we have the ability to not ever have reality again. We
never need to ever see the *Mona Lisa* in reality, as we have it in our own home. In
fact, just as we prefer Disneyland's main street, we will prefer the atomic printed
Mona Lisa. Furthermore, imagine a thief switching the atomic printed *Mona Lisa*
for the 'real' one. Would we know? Will there even be such thing as "the" *Mona
Lisa* in the future? In the fourth order that question doesn't matter – the real one
is the one we can all have, in its multiplicity. Multiplicity (as fractals) is the reality principle over singularity (originality). Anything can be made anywhere all
the time – our notion of context has disappeared, or forgotten in futures where
everyone has the same. We never even need to make anything new again – it is
all already made, one just chooses when and where to have it surround them. As

we proceed, our experiences are never real or not real – our experience of life will always be 'up for debate' – reality will always have a fractal existence meaning the further we look 'into' it, the more of the same we see.

6   The Dark Art of Deepfakes

Another contemporary example would be what are called 'deepfakes.' These are simulations that fool visual and audio senses; they 'fool' a human being's biological systems in order to 'fake' reality to such an extent as to be reality. For example, audio and video can be simulated for any voice or person. In political races opponents can create a fake video and audio of the opponent saying/ doing horrible things and people will not be able to tell the difference with their senses alone. Because we still make symbolic values, a reality of 'deepfakes' is not only possible but inevitable (in fact, a simple Google search will turn up millions of results). These developments are suggestive of a world that can say and do anything in any context. There is no origin as they are completely made from reconfiguring bits of context. They are truly the simulation which functions from the precession of simulation. In other words, we use the simulation function to subvert itself, and place deepfakes into the simulation to further erode realities. In essence, our biology cannot discern the difference between these fakes and something we sense as real. Once deepfakes are placed into our everyday operations of life we can imagine an experience in which everything can happen or has happened at any time. We can reverse history, fake any event, create total immersion into any reality – as your body cannot tell the difference physically and neurologically. In the future any connection we had to being able to make sense, use our senses, or have embodied experiences can be faked. The ability to say an event really happened will disappear, as all events can happen. It is only a matter programming. Once that program is put into the circulation of what we tether to reality, it joins the function of the simulation and the disappearance of our ability to pin down one reality over another. This *algorithmic turn of reality* is Baudrillard's nightmare.

7   Algorithmic Life and Fractal Futures

> The permanent lie is the apotheosis of totalitarianism. It no longer matters what is true. It matters only what is 'correct.' (Hedges, 2018)

Baudrillard (2012) asserted that the screen is replacing the scene. Now, the internet and the algorithmic processes serve as the process of life (as life), which continue to grow in influence and physical proximity to our experiences exponentially. Baudrillard foresaw a world much like the one unfolding in front of us, even if hidden in algorithms or codes that have become 'black boxes' – meaning we don't know how they work – but use them all day, every day. We are ever more drawn into a world made by black boxes and rely on their implicit functioning to interact with each other. The actual rhythms of social media, Amazon Prime, Google searches, and culture on demand via Netflix or YouTube functions as part of the simulation with the potential to do even more damage as they become purely algorithmic. We no longer move to the rhythm of life, but the algorithm of life. As we move away from the old ways in which reality was experienced, and into increasingly sophisticated simulation, there are consequences in the domains we have labeled economics, politics, education, etc., basically all social systems are becoming/could become algorithmic.

One might say that algorithms are simply pre-selected outcomes given the input of data, what's the problem if we make life better and more efficient? But we are increasingly pressured to use algorithms to reveal the 'correct code' for 'living' or 'doing.' This doing results in ever more maps or codes to form realities and actions that affect our everyday lives. One example is when politicians use algorithms to select voters via gerrymandering. This system results in outcomes for more and more districts predetermined by algorithms for the candidate to win by selected demography rather than trying to win over voters via political persuasion – the 'voting maps' truly precedes the territory. Politics has changed from trying to persuade people to vote for you into selecting voter maps to make sure you can win. Another general example is information control (or code control). Information about the world is being written in the code of the corporate elite, the oligarchs of power shaping reality – manufacturing consent in the 21st century. As Buyniski (2018) explains, Wikipedia is not written but controlled as a simulation of an encyclopedia. Simulated capitalism, the total algorithmic rhythm of our surroundings, deepfakes, fake news, post truth, post politics, etc., has taken the place of so-called reality. Life has truly imitated these arts. This algorithmic homogenization of the world, its flattening (and disappearance) as codes that 'make correct' that which is outside of the norm, outside of the chosen reality code is what Baudrillard's work on simulation and proposal for fatal theory hopes to point out and strategize resistance to, which we will examine in the final chapter.

Notes

1 This idea connects to neuroscience's findings – in fact we hallucinate reality – we use the information entering our sensory system and create reality – we are in essence drafts-people – we are 'lying' in a sense to ourselves about the world.

2   This aesthetic dimension will not be fully developed in this chapter, but could be connected
    to fatal theory explored in the final chapter.
3   Introduced in the *Transparency of Evil* (2009, p. 5) this fourth order is not accepted by all
    scholars of Baudrillard. In fact, Butler (1999) does not distinguish it from the third, while for
    Gane (2000) it is a new stage. We, especially given the current 'order,' support a reading of a
    fourth order in Gane.
4   Imaging 3D printing technology, Virtual Reality, Augmented Reality, etc. being distributed by
    Disney and personalize parks in each place can be made – in essence Disney is a fractal code.
5   In neuroscience the brain's primary function is to model reality for us. As mentioned before,
    we create reality in our visual, auditory, and colorful experiences from information gathered
    by our bodies in the world. Baudrillard might say that neuroscience itself is a model, a pre-
    cursor to any real grasping of reality, thus always putting us back into the precession of sim-
    ulation.

References

Baudrillard, J. (1994). *Simulacra and simulation* (S. Fisher, Trans). University of Michi-
    gan Press. (Original work published in 1981)
Baudrillard, J. (2009). *Transparency of evil: Essays on extreme phenomena*. Verso Books.
Baudrillard, J. (2012). *The ecstasy of communication*. Semiotext(e).
Butler, R. (1999). *Jean Baudrillard: The defence of the real*. Sage.
Buyniski, H. (2018, October 20). *On contact: Wikipedia—A tool of the ruling elite* [Video].
    YouTube. https://www.youtube.com/watch?v=nDPrpKDjQ5U
Delanty, G. (Ed.). (2004). *Volume 3: Social theory & the critique on modernity: Part 3:
    Popular culture and capitalism*. Sage Publications Ltd.
Gane, M. (2000). *Jean Baudrillard: In radical uncertainty*. Pluto Press.
Hardwick, M. J. (2004). *Mall maker: Victor Gruen, architect of an American dream*. Uni-
    versity of Pennsylvania Press.
Hedges, C. (2006). *American fascists*. Free Press.
Hedges, C. (2009). *Empire of Illusion*. Nation Books.
Hedges, C. (2017, December 17). The permanent lie, our deadliest threat. *Truthdig*.
    https://www.truthdig.com/articles/permanent-lie-deadliest-threat/
Jones, J. (2018, October 14). The Da Vinci mystery: Why is his $450m masterpiece really
    being kept under wraps? *The Guardian*. https://www.theguardian.com/artandde-
    sign/2018/oct/14/leonardo-da-vinci-mystery-why-is-his-450m-masterpiece-really-
    being-kept-under-wraps-salvator-mundi
Telecommunications Act of 1996, Pub. LA. No. 104-104, 110 Stat. 56. (1996). Federal
    Communications Commission. https://www.fcc.gov/general/telecommunications-
    act-1996
Wilde, O. (1891). The decay of lying: An observation. In *Intentions* (pp. 1–56). Meu-
    then & Co.

CHAPTER 4

Fatal Theory and Education

> Philosophers have hitherto only interpreted the world in various ways; the point is to change it.
>
> MARX (1998, p. 574)

•••

> It may be that Marx's famous eleventh thesis on Feuerbach – the central pillar of the revolutionary methodology of the last century and a half – simply needs to be overturned.
>
> BERARDI (2019, p. 3)

∵

Along with the vast majority of other philosophers of the 20th century (and into the first quarter of the 21st), philosophers of education have taken to heart Marx's (1998) famous quote above. Insofar as it is connected to critical thought, dialectic critique, and critical theory, the eleventh thesis is no match for a world of simulation; a world of deepfakes and algorithms. It is intellectually anachronistic in a world of the perfect crime – the world's virtual double – and the fourth order of simulacra. In fact, Berardi (2019) goes on to say of philosophers having tried to enact the eleventh thesis, "The results are catastrophic." We have noted the inefficaciousness of traditional critique in previous chapters and introduced some of Baudrillard's responses to that impotence including dispensation with critical thought and the adoption of radical thought and the trading of critical theory for theory-fiction. Another way of saying this is that Baudrillard's responses to the inefficacy of traditional critique/critical thought/critical theory are what constitute fatal theory. Beradi gives us another response that is, in a sense, an overarching category under which Baudrillard's responses to the third and fourth orders of simulacra fall. He says,

> The philosopher's task is not to change the world – the world continually changes with no need of philosophers. The philosopher's task is to inter-

© KONINKLIJKE BRILL NV, LEIDEN, 2021 | DOI: 10.1163/9789004445376_005

pret the world, that is, to capture its tendency and above all to enunciate the possibilities inscribed therein. (Berardi, 2019, p. 3)

We think Baudrillard would have agreed, wholeheartedly, with Berardi on this point – particularly if the interpretation is done anagrammatically, with myth and theory-fiction, with metaphor and aphorism.

Berardi's call for philosophers to treat the interpretation of the world as their primordial task is consistent with Baudrillard's fatal theory. In this final chapter, we sketch out, in broad strokes, a fatal theory for education. We do this by discussing a vision of *ars moriendi* and *amor fati* for education and then by placing Baudrillard's tools for fatal theory, namely, radical thought, theory-fiction, thought experiments, etc. in the context of philosophy of education. We will not exhaust the possible ways in which Baudrillard's fatal theory can be put into conversation with philosophy of education in this short chapter. Much like the entire guidebook, this chapter on fatal theory and education is not meant to be comprehensive. It is, rather, meant to spark a conversation about the possible relationship between Baudrillard's description of and response to the fourth order of simulacra and educational philosophy. It is highly unlikely that such a conversation will result in philosophers of education abandoning the Greeks, the Enlightenment philosophers, John Dewey and other American pragmatists, critical theorists, etc., nor is it the case that such an abandonment would be necessary in terms of the goals of our current project. What is necessary for the conversation is that Baudrillard's fatal theory be seriously considered in light of philosophical problems and inquiry that have something to say about education. That is, philosophy of education, as an academic field and as a practice, should consider seriously fatal theory as an intellectual tradition with something to contribute to the ongoing conversations in philosophy of education – something every bit as legitimate as the other traditions that currently dominate those conversations.

Taking inspiration from Baudrillard himself and a number of Baudrillardian scholars, we begin our sketch of fatal theory for education with discussions of *ars moriendi*, or, the art of dying and *amor fati*, or, the love of fate, before moving on to a discussion of Baudrillard's fatal strategies of theory-fiction, radical thought, thought experiments, and aphorisms.

1   *Ars Moriendi* for Education

… the highest values are losing their value. (Nietzsche, 2019, p. 12)

Ars moriendi or books on the 'art of dying' where one of the first literary rages of the 15th century. These texts, appearing on the heals of the black death, and among the first printed books, illustrated with block prints, and were written to instruct people how to die (Beaty, 1970). In essence there was an art to dying. It wasn't simply a thing that happens to you, but an event that needed to be thought out, planned, *strategized*. In essense, there is an aesthetic dimension that should be added, or lived though (undergone) in order to die artfully.

Leaving the *ars moriendi* behind in all but metaphor, how can we attach the concerns for dying nicely with Baudrillard's fatal theory? It seems what is fatal about theory, Baudrillard's worst nightmare, is that we do nothing. Or perhaps one might say that we continue to do nothing differently. We continue to let the theories, critical or otherwise, that have guided our strategy for changing the world unfold without any reckoning. As we have noted, this path has led us not to changing the world in the radical way required for emancipation, regardless of Pinker's (2019) latest thesis, but as noted by Berardi, theory needs to interpret a fractal reality that blocks critical theories from emancipatory practice before they can even begin to propose them.

Returning to the metaphor as *ars moriendi*, we suggest a reading of Baudrillard in which he gives us the guidebook, or fatal strategy, for theory to die. For if we do not plan for or strategize how to die nicely, then we will die with the theories that have given us the Anthropocene. To be complicit in ideologies of the Anthropocene, à la Žižek (2008), is still doing something. If we do nothing in a Baudrillardian sense we just continue to let the world disappear, allow the 'fractalized' fourth order of simulacra to replace reality, and never address deterrence of reality, etc. then not only can we argue, for example, that the critical theory of the Frankfurt School failed, but that these ideas, because of the claims made and impossible practice proposed by them, has in fact given us the Anthropocene.

This is a key point and one that, given the current context of philosophy of education, should be heeded. We have seen a massive erosion of public education in terms of its effectiveness to create a just society and healthy democratic paticipation in the United States and the factors are many. Neoliberal economics, ideologies of infividualism, post-political apathy, post-truth, etc. are all culprits.[1] The question might be asked given all of the emancipatory strategies, critical and social theories, educational solutions which allegedly result in equity etc., why has the situation in education in the United State become so calibrated for the Anthropocene? (see Ravitch's triology, 2010, 2013, 2020, for a chronicle of this issue in detail). Why do we not have a politics, ethical commitments, democratic participation, or frankly a discourse which confers upon the population a sense of community given the diverse needs of our society?

Instead of those modern theories that have bequeathed us the Anthropocene, Baudrillard (1990) prefers to take the side of the object. That sounds like an awkward thing to say, siding with the 'object.' But the object for Baudrillard means something interesting. Baudrillard, like a lot of late 20th century thinkers, wades into the subject-object distinction in Western philosophy. This Cartesian construction, sets subjects apart from objects, or subjectivities' (our selves) relationships with the world (object). However this distinction or binary bleeds all over the place with the cuts from post-structuralist thinkers. The torture of the subject-object distinction has been done with precision by many schools of philosophy since its inception. What Baudrillard adds is his insistence on thinking through this construction by imagining the agency of the object.

Given that the subject of power, knowledge, or history cannot be assumed, "[t]he only strategy possible is that of the object" (Baudrillard, 1990, p. 143). Baudrillard is interested here in taking the position of the object. In this context, he uses "[s]tories of reversibility." In particular, he uses the story of the rat and the psychologist, told from the point of view of the rat (read = object) explaining, "[T]he rat tells about how he ended up by perfectly conditioning the psychologist to give him a piece of bread every time he lifted the gate of his cage" (1990, p. 112). This is Baudrillard's idea of the revenge of the object. "[Y]ou could imagine ... that the experiment would have been faked – not involuntarily altered by the observer, but faked by the object ..." (p. 112). There is something in the position of the object that defies the subject and this is what Baudrillard was seeking out. Pawlett has picked up on Baudrillard's siding with the object. Pawlett (2007) says, "The strategies of the object are experienced as ironic because they subvert the supposed mastery or sovereignty of the subject, ironic because indifferent to the wishes of the subject" (p. 114). Pawlett points out that, for Baudrillard, talk of the object also, in a sense, *includes* the subject. "According to Baudrillard, we all live in ambivalence as *both* subject *and* object, both self and other" (p. 114).

The point here is that part of *ars moriendi*, as a condition of fatal theory, must include this subject/object ambivalence as opposed to the 'arrogant glory' of the metaphysics of the subject (Baudrillard, 1990). Such a metaphysics is part and parcel of the Anthropocene and critical theories. After all, it is the emancipation of subjects, not objects, that is sought in critical philosophies. Baudrillard would suggest that in our construction of an intertwined subject-object the failure of critical theory is not only in its empirical sense, but even if it has succeeded it would fail again because only the subject's relationship would be emancipated. Objects would still be subject to mediation or domination under a new regime of the subject.

But it can also be said that the subject/object ambivalence is of particular use in dying artfully in philosophy of education. If we can consider education (in whatever definitional context) an object of observation, study, inquiry, then this object has surely exacted revenge on the subject. In philosophy of education, there are myriad ways to think of the object (education) as having subverted the mastery or sovereignty of the subject (the philosopher). Part of dying artfully for a philosopher of education is to countenance this revenge of the object as opposed to dying in a blaze of arrogant glory. If, perhaps, the end is nigh for philosophy of education, progressive education, education for democracy, critical pedagogy, etc., (or at least death is imminent in their current forms) then we must begin to take the position of the object, to consider the revenge of education *qua* object, and embrace our own subject/object ambivalence. That is, if we are to die artfully.

The representation of death in the *ars moriendi* books symbolized the impossibility of representation of death and instead give us a kind of fatal theory of death. But perhaps we should disregard the notion of theory altogether because theory does not work in reality – it is part of the problem of reality. The model of theory, the code of theory (critical, reason, see Chapter 2) must be radically undone – or even not done – in order to change the circumstances of our events. Thus the 'art of dying' must proceed the 'act of dying'; or its art must proceed life (simulation from Chapter 3).

We began this section with a quote from Nietzsche (2019), "the highest values are losing their value" (p. 12) because his words have bearing on the course of an art of dying or in Baudrillardian terms a fatal strategy – and for our purposes we add, fatal strategy for the philosophy of education. This quote refers to the theory of value – or transvaluation the needs to be undergone, not overcome (in the Janicaudian sense). Transvaluation – the re-evaluation of all values – needs fatal theory – or we could combine a Nietzschian transvaluation as fatal theory to combat simulation, fractal reality – the reality we have 'now.'

2   *Amor Fati*: Embracing Fatal Theory in Education

Fatal theory in education cannot end with the concept dying artfully, though. As we mentioned earlier, according to Baudrillard, radical thought – a key component of his fatal theory – is never depressive. It is in this milieu that we argue that fatal theory for education involves the confluence of *ars moriendi* with *amor fati*, or, love of fate. Nietzsche's *amor fati* is associated with his concept of eternal recurrence, the idea that one should live one's life as if she or he would have to live it over and over again – infinitely – the exact same way (Nietzsche, 2001). But *amor fati* does not necessarily have to confine itself to life events. It can also include accepting one's fate in terms of who one is (not just subject but also object, perhaps). Nietzsche's idea here was to embrace who one is, without cowering from, ignoring, or seeking to mute the more disastrous parts of ourselves and our lives. American philosopher John Kaag (2018) has recently put Nietzsche's ideas here together with one of Nietzsche's earlier readers, Herman Hesse, in a book written for a more popular audience.

Kaag (2018) describes Hesse as a reader of Nietzsche, though not a disciple. Hesse's departure from Nietzsche was mostly connected to Nietzsche's concept of master morality but he found commonality with Nietzsche around the notion of a fractured self (we can imagine for our purposes, a self in which there is a kind of subject/object ambivalence). "Hesse's interest in Nietzsche ratcheted up ... as he began to address the fate of the divided self" (Kaag, 2018, p. 199). Kaag is referring to Hesse's (1929) *Steppenwolf*. In the novel, Harry Haller's manuscript is discovered and published. The manuscript reveals that the middle-aged Harry harbors concerns about his fitness for everyday bourgeois society because he recognizes in himself a disposition in contrast to the refined veneer he puts on for his everyday interactions. He realizes, underneath it, he is a 'hairy howler' – like the wolf of the Steppes.

The last part of Hesse's (1929) novel takes place in "The Magic Theatre" – Kaag (2018) describes it as "a metaphorical funhouse of his mind, filled with doors and mirrors and characters from his almost forgotten past. What lies beneath the surface of Haller's life? ... It turns out it isn't just the Steppenwolf ... It is more insane, but also more hopeful than that" (Kaag, 2018, p. 207). It is more insane because Haller's subconscious turns out to be full of orgiastic and murderous impulses. It is more hopeful because his judgment for being a divided self is that he is 'to live.' His 'executioners' declare, "As if there were not enough unhappiness in all you have designed already! However, enough of pathos and death-dealing. It is time to come to your senses. You are to live and to learn to laugh" (Hesse, 1929, p. 216).

This is a much too brief introduction to Nietzsche's (Hesse's) *amor fati*. That said, the embracing of one's fate as a divided self or as subject/object ambivalence is part of what might form a fatal theory in education, taken together with *ars moriendi*. In philosophy of education, perhaps we can both learn how to die artfully, taking the position of the object as well as loving and embracing our fate as both subject and object, as both refined and impulsive, as both human and wolf of the Steppes. In this way, we can learn to die artfully, in part, by putting an end to pathos and learning to live and laugh. This is the philosopher of education as fatal theorist – taking the position of the object of education and embracing our fate of ambivalent subject/object in our philosophical pursuit.

Kaag's (2018) translation of Haller's lesson in *amor fati* is "not to 'get a grip' but to loosen one's hold" (p. 214). This is consistent with Baudrillard's later work, after having established himself as the preeminent theorist of consumption (and later) simulation. That is to say, he, developed a number of fatal strategies, perhaps the primary one being a kind of fading away as a writing subject via style and form. Pawlett (2007) describes his later writing this way, "Baudrillard would no longer assume the secure position as *knower*, of the leading theorist of consumption or of simulation" (p. 109). Instead, he wrote theory-fiction, theory-diaries, aphorisms, and published photographs. However, as Pawlett points out, the aphorism for Baudrillard is "not an exercise in the writing of postmodern fragmentation" but rather, "a quintessentially modernist literary device" that Baudrillard associates with "'cerebral electricity' recall[ing] Woolf and Joyce as much as Nietzsche" (2007, pp. 108–109). But after dying artfully and disappearing as a knowing subject, Baudrillard as theorist did not disappear. As previously noted, and supported by the work the preeminent Baudrillard scholar, Gane (2000), Baudrillard as fatal theorist retains a systematicity. Pawlett (2007) describes it this way, "Baudrillard apparently begins a second life, a life after subjectivity, after desire, after his greatest successes ... Nevertheless, he continued to theorise ..." (p. 109).

3   Fatal Theory or Fatal Strategy: The Baudrillard Experience

> ... the result of a consistent and total substitution of lies for factual truth is not that the lie will now be accepted as truth, and truth be defamed as lies, but that the sense by which we take our bearings in the real world—and the category of truth vs. falsehood is among the mental means to this end—is being destroyed. (Arendt, 1967, p. 257)

Arendt wrote this in the 1950s to address the use of lies and truth in politics. Here we can put this issue to work considering Badurillard's fatal strategy. Ardent's work sought to address the loss of meaning of concepts like reason, truth, justice ,etc., which has seemingly exponentially exploded in our current age. Her approach was to use the tools of philosophy and to analyze and 'exercise' the reader in order to bring them to a critical consciousness of the problem with the hopes of addressing and overcoming them. To evoke Janicaud once more an 'undergoing' not an overcoming strategy is needed. We must undergo and in fact deploy these post-truth phenomena in order to truly combat them. We must assume the position of the object, create and experience the fictions, emancipate ourselves from control of the code to be infected by them in order for the virus of a fatal theory to emerge. In short, for Baudrillard, when facing a world that is unintelligible and problematic, our task is clear: we must make that world even more unintelligible, even more enigmatic (2001, p. 83). This was certainly not Arendt's solution, but it is Baudrillard's.

We argue that in order to understand fatal theory or fatal strategies, one must understand the experience Baudrillard's work becomes. As stated previously, Baudrillard seems to give up his own power in his writing and lets himself become a vehicle for rhetoric and style of what on the surface becomes for some (especially philsophers) unintelligible. But here the shift in philosophical writing is important to understand and is a sticking point for people beginning to try to read Badurillard. The point is not to understand writing as a refelction of truth, but understand writing as another infected code that had been compromised, or implicated in the murder of reality. Writing for Baudrillard is a virus that reality can hinge upon. We must experience the tension of a writing that refused to directly address the situation, and in fact we must experience writing as the impossibility to 'make sense.' Writing became a fatal strategy in the hands of Baudrillard and it is important to note that his attempt to split our ability to form reality in the classic sense of representation is given over to simulation as addressed in Chapter 3.

Thus we have Baudrillard writing a fatal strategy, but the writing is teaching the reader a new way to read and to exist with writing. Baudrillard is suggesting that a new reading, a kind of reading that we learn in adverstining and post-truth simulation realities (as noted and warned by Ardent above) will lead us to a fatal theory to undergo the fractal reality with which we presently find ourselves coping. Writing no longer is concerned with lies and truth, but with the *operation* of truth vs. falsehood. This operation had changed, like the operation of writing and philosophy. No longer is writing realted linearly to truth, *nor can writing be the linear practice of philosophy*. As Baudrillard recalibrated writing he also recalibrated philosophy or theortical practice. In the fractal world, we require a fractal practice of philosophy. Let's examine this from another angle.

In order to practice theory in our age it seems to be quite simple – think of everything as an advertisement. Or think of the terrain of truth infected by the virus of the architecture of persuasion that advertising in our culture now privileges. Thus we have the decay of truth into an advertising campaign; in which facts have to be lobbied to be believed resulting in a 'delay' in truth. That is, we cannot make up our minds about what the truth vs. falsehood (as Arendt, 1967, worried about) *operation* is, not what is literally true or false.

As we are assaulted with alternative facts and multiple sets of realities, or truths, and the displacement of truth by the multiple realities becomes the new default setting of 'reality,' we arrive within the Baudrillard experience. In other words, truth as simulation does not have to function in terms of an operation of representation in writing of a truth. Instead truth circulates, it is never tethered to anything – like conspiracy theories and pyramid schemes which have become 'reality' in our context. This results is a certain kind of chaos. And Berardi (2019) says, "Those who wage war on chaos will be defeated because chaos feeds upon war ... chaos is stronger than order. So the best thing to do is to make friends with chaos" (pp. 1–3). This is the task of the philosopher of education as fatal theorist and fatal strategist.

4   Fatal Strategies for Education: Learning the Art of Dying, Loving Fate, and Making Friends with Chaos

In Chapter 3, we quoted Oscar Wilde's (1899) assertion via his fictional essay that life imitated art. We wished to evoke a poetic way in which to begin to unravel the assumptions that build reality. These assumptions stand in the way of changing reality in a meaningful way. Fatal theory could be learning to master the art of dying, or to become aware that reailty's death needs a guide (fatal strategy) in order to 'live dying.' To live within a dying world is to create new opportunities and a new impetus to interpret it. In a world without an 'outside,' without a critical theory's ability to change the world, only fatal strategies of interpretation can 'work.' Perhaps Baudrillard's fatal theory is just such a phenomenon for education, but it comes with a price.

Once upon a time, reality was correspondent to truth. Now, after the procession of the simulacra, according to Baudrillard, we have not multi-reality, but simulation, a leveling of realities. Everything is actualized and because of this, reality corresponds not to representations, but exceeds them, it ping-pongs back from each moment of truth, or makes representation a quaint remnant of the Enlightenment. We now have circulation of truth and moments when it appears tethered to reality only to experience a moment later that connection has severed. How do we undergo these trajectories of 'reality'? How do we experience chaos and wield its power to destroy itself?

Philosophers of education have, by and large, not accepted or responded to what is described above – the fourth order of simulacrum. As a field, philosophy of education only rarely exhibits a relationship to *amor fati* and *ars moriendi*. Philosophers of education have eschewed making friends with chaos and instead insisted on mastering their object through critical thought and critical theory. But, Baudrillard's twofold gift to us (one that keeps on giving as we continue to move toward the perfect crime and the full virtualization of the world) is (1) the description of the world as a place where such activity as is standard for philosophers of education is ineffectual and (2) the prescription for pushing back against such a world must be thought within the ineffectual, not the critical or literal. We must return the world's enigmatic state with more enigma. We must make friends with chaos.

Enigma and chaos are not typically embraced by philosophers of education but as we move closer and closer to integral reality, we must consider fatal theory and fatal strategies that include an engagement with radical thought, which, "wagers on the illusion of the world." (Baudrillard, 2008, p. 98). In so doing, writing must take on different forms. As noted previously, for Baudrillard this included a kind of theory-fiction diary (or the type of writing strategy we described above), and aphorisms. These are modes by which he thought writing could accomplish its task of returning enigma with more enigma. "Whatever its object, writing must make the illusion of that object shine forth, must make it an impenetrable enigma ... The objective of writing is to alter its object ... Writing aims at a total resolution – a poetic resolution" (Baudrillard, 2008, p. 101). This kind of writing is scarce in philosophy of education and we argue that this is in part due to the field's non-relationship with *ars moriendi* and *amor fati* – its dearth of fatal theory. Philosophy of education typically charges this kind of writing as nihilistic but as we have mentioned in multiple places in this guidebook, Baudrillard has refuted that claim. Still, what is the alternative to writing that is charged as depressive? He said, "At any rate, better a despairing analysis in felicitous language than an optimistic analysis in an infelicitous language that is maddeningly tedious and demoralizingly platitudinous, as is most often the case" (Baudrillard, 2008, p. 104). One potential future project for our field would be to find, create and archive Badurillaridan spaces of writing for philosophy of education.

Fatal theory and fatal strategies for philosophy of education must include a different kind of writing, one that avoids the pitfall of becoming 'demoralizingly platitudinous,' and, rather, submits itself as a friend to chaos. Instead of seeking to master its object it must be writing that illuminates the illusion of that object – and there is much to illuminate as illusory in education. It is a kind of writing that must be informed by thought that is radical (as opposed to critical), that "has to be exceptional, anticipatory, and at the margin – has to be the projected shadow of future events. Today we are lagging behind events" (Baudrillard, 2008, p. 102). One of the events that philosophers of education are lagging behind is the death of philosophy of education. In order to die artfully, love our fate, and indeed, we must disappear and 'begin a second life' – we must enact fatal strategies.[2] This collects the courage to hoist the ineffable, undergo chaos, and experience rather than read Jean Baudrillard.

Notes

1 Without the space to fully articulate this point, constructivsm might be a particular case to think through in education with Baudrillard.
2 For a rare example of writing in philosophy of education that approximates the fatal strategies outlined above, see Allen (2017).

References

Allen, A. (2017). *The cynical educator*. MayFly Books.

Arendt, H. (1967, February 18). Truth and politics. *The New Yorker*, p. 49.

Baudrillard, J. (1990). *Fatal strategies*. Pluto Press.

Baudrillard, J. (2001). *Vital illusion*. Columbia University Press.

Baudrillard, J. (2008). *The perfect crime*. Verso Books.

Beaty, N. L. (1970). *The craft of dying: A study in the literary tradition of the ars moriendi in England*. Yale University Press.

Berardi, F. (2019). *The second coming*. Polity Press.

Hesse, H. (1929). *Steppenwolf*. Henry Holt & Co.

Kaag, J. (2018). *Hiking with Nietzsche: On becoming who you are*. Farrar, Straus, and Giroux.

Marx, K. (1998). *The German ideology, including theses on feuerbach and the introduction to the critique of political economy*. Prometheus Books.

Nietzsche, F. (2001). *The gay science: With prelude in German rhymes and an appendix of songs* (J. Nauckhoff, Trans.). University Press.

Nietzsche, F. (2019). *The will to power* (Vols. I and II) (A. Ludovici, Trans.). Digireads. com Publishing.

Pawlett, W. (2007). *Jean Baudrillard: Against banality*. Routledge.

Pinker, S. (2019). *Enlightenment now: The case for reason, science, humanism, and progress*. Penguin Books.

Ravitch, D. (2010). *The death and life of the great American school system: How testing and choice are undermining education*. Basic Books.

Ravitch, D. (2013). *Reign of error: The hoax of the privatization movement and the danger to America's public schools*. Vintage Books.

Ravitch, D. (2020). *Slaying Goliath: The passionate resistance to privitization and the fight to sace America's public schools*. Alfred Knopf.

Žižek, S. (2008). *Violence*. Picador.

Index

www.ingramcontent.com/pod-product-compliance
Lightning Source LLC
Chambersburg PA
CBHW050526280326
41932CB00014B/2479